# THOM & JOANI SCHULTZ

# CREATIVE FAITH AH-HA'S!

## 45 EXPERIENCES TO ENRICH YOUTH IN MINISTRY

**Group**

Loveland, Colorado

# DEDICATION

## To Matt,
our son and God's gift, who always inspires us, amuses us, surprises us, and loves us.

## To Glen and Kathy Schlecht,
who dared to dream of ways to involve our church's youth in new and exciting ways. Not only is Glen a great pastor and Kathy a great music minister, they're both great friends!

*Creative Faith Ah-Ha's:*
*45 Experiences to Enrich Youth in Ministry*

Copyright © 2004 Thom and Joani Schultz

Visit our Web site: **www.grouppublishing.com**

### CREDITS

Editor: Paul Woods

Creative Development Editor: Kelli B. Trujillo

Chief Creative Officer: Joani Schultz

Copy Editor: Lyndsay E. Gerwing

Book Designer: Jean Bruns

Print Production Artist: Helen Harrison

Cover Art Director/Designer: Jeff A. Storm

Illustrator: Lynn Rowe Reed

Production Manager: Peggy Naylor

Unless otherwise noted, Scripture taken from the HOLY BIBLE, NEW INTERNATIONAL VERSION®. Copyright © 1973, 1978, 1984 by International Bible Society. Used by permission of Zondervan Publishing House. All rights reserved.

### LIBRARY OF CONGRESS CATALOGING-IN-PUBLICATION DATA

Schultz, Thom.

Creative faith ah-ha's : 45 experiences to enrich youth in ministry / by Thom and Joani Schultz.—1st American pbk. ed.

    p. cm.

Includes index.

ISBN 0-7644-2619-2 (pbk. : alk. paper)

1. Church group work with youth. 2. Active learning. 3. Experiential learning. I. Schultz, Joani, 1953-
II. Title.

BV4447.S348 2003

259'.2—dc22                            2003015057

10 9 8 7 6 5 4 3 2 1     13 12 11 10 09 08 07 06 05 04

Printed in the United States of America.

# TABLE OF CONTENTS

# CHAPTER ONE

# A NEW APPROACH TO AN OLD PROGRAM

The kids hated to come. Our church's weekly coming-of-age doctrinal program consistently accomplished one thing: It soured kids on church. The old ritualistic program taught kids—unintentionally—that church was boring, irrelevant, and unappetizing.

But many of the parents and other older congregation members *revered* the old program. "If it was good enough for me when I was a kid, it's good enough for these kids today," they'd say. That attitude perpetuated an old system for generations. Hundreds of kids, through many decades, endured the weekly drudgery of dry teacher lectures, rote memorization, and school-like tests.

A study of the church's statistics revealed that a high percentage of the kids dropped out of church participation as soon as they "graduated" from the program. The program that was supposed to confirm the kids' faith and plug them into church life was producing precisely the opposite effect.

## A NEW VISION

Our pastor was ready to buck tradition and seek a new way of doing this ministry. He wanted results. He wanted to hold on to these kids. He wanted to see their faith come alive. So we sat down together with him to dream a new vision. (Incidentally, we had a heightened interest because our young son, Matt, was about to enter this program.)

We formed a planning team with interested parents and their middle school–aged kids. And rather than beginning with a critique of the old program, we asked why we're doing what we're doing. What's the purpose of this program? What are its goals? We were afraid that some of the parents, who had been through the program themselves as young teenagers, would see the purpose tied to perpetuating the old program for its own sake. We were wrong. They, and their kids, saw a higher, more important goal.

After plenty of discussion, the planning group agreed on this purpose statement:

*To establish a lifelong relationship*
*with a growing commitment*
*to Jesus Christ,*
*which builds faith, hope, and joy*
*for our daily lives.*

You see, we realized that the real goal of this program was not to process Bible facts, memorize words, or survive a grilling by church elders. The real goal was to weave a loving relationship with Jesus. We now could begin designing a new program aimed at meeting this goal.

The planning team envisioned what the new program might look like—and what it shouldn't look like. We came up with an "in" list and an "out" list. Here's how it looked:

| *What's In* | *What's Out* |
| --- | --- |
| Excitement | Boring |
| Fun | Have-to's |
| Enrichment | Unemotional |
| Relevance | Dry |
| Activities | Lectures |
| Fellowship | Useless |
| Discussion | memorization |
| Bible study | Sitting, just |
| Prayer | listening |
| Interaction | Rigid, harsh |
| Relationships | |
| Understanding | |
| Service | |
| Family involvement | |
| Learn by doing | |
| Different settings | |

The more we talked, the more excited everyone became. Maybe we really could design a program in which young people would actually want to participate. Maybe it could be appealing enough that they would actually want to bring their friends (which was unheard of before).

# A NEW DESIGN

We sensed that building a relationship with Jesus bears a real resemblance to building a relationship with another person. We grow closer to God through some of the same means by which we grow closer to a friend or relative. We used our new purpose statement as a filter for all ideas and possible new structures for our program. If an element didn't help to build a warm relationship with Jesus, it didn't belong.

We realized many of the old program's elements would never be used to build a relationship with anyone. Nobody pursues a real friendship through boring lectures, fill-in-the-blank worksheets, passive sitting, or trivial quizzes.

Our new program contains a variety of elements—all designed to build a friendship with Jesus. The design includes some pieces that remain consistent each week. Other elements change regularly. And some features are one-time special events. Here's what we designed:

- *Focused opening*. Each week the pastor gathers everyone for a fifteen-minute kickoff based on the theme of the week.

- *Weekly small groups*. We form same-gender groups of four to six kids and one adult to focus on a prepared Scripture study each week. Group participants also spend time sharing the highlights and lowlights of their week with one another. And they devote a good amount of time to praying—for one another and for any concerns that arise during their discussion. This is a natural time of friendship-building—with one another and with Jesus. Small groups meet for fifty minutes each week. The pastor assigns the small groups, and adults for the small groups are chosen for their faith maturity and their love of young people.

- *Creative worship tracks*. We devote thirty minutes per week to creative worship tracks. Every month or so, kids choose from a list of experiences to enrich their faith and contribute to the life of the church. These three- to

six-week series appeal to a variety of interests, gifts, and abilities. Many of these experiences result in students contributing to the church's regular congregational worship services. This book describes these "ah-ha" worship experiences in detail.

- *Special events*. We designed special events that allowed more time to explore some topics in depth. These experiences occur during an overnight retreat, an all-day Saturday event, or a special series over a period of weeks. During these times the kids discover Jesus through explorations of baptism, the Lord's Supper, stewardship, the Lord's Prayer, and so on. We've included details of our baptism special event in this book.

Our program happens on Wednesday nights, and we include a meal for the kids each week. Parents and other congregation members are invited to join the kids for the meal. We experimented with a guided discussion at the dinner tables, but the kids told us that was too much structure. They needed some undirected time to hang out with their friends and families.

So, now that the new approach to an old program has been running a few years, what are the results? Well, the young people give it high scores. Some of the old-line adults still pine for the old ways. But the students who have completed the program, including our son, Matt, have grown closer to Christ, to one another, and to their church.

That's what we were looking for.

# CHAPTER TWO

# WHY AND HOW FAITH AH-HA'S WORK

We've collected in this book a cornucopia of Faith Ah-Ha's—experiences designed to help your teenagers discover the heart of Jesus and grow closer to him. We refer to these as creative worship experiences. Some are designed to blend into your church's regular congregational worship times. Others unfold at other times and in other settings. But they all fit the description of worship. In fact, we like to remind kids that worship is not limited to Sunday morning. We worship God whenever we reflect on his awesome love for us, praise him, give thanks, and seek to grow closer to him.

These Ah-Ha's work. They're tested and tweaked for best results. The factors that follow are some of the reasons they work. These Ah-Ha's incorporate authentic learning, or what we often call REAL™ learning. That stands for Relational, Experiential, Applicable, and Learner-based. We've found this REAL approach leads to a bonding friendship with Jesus, deeper learning, stickier retention, and more potent life application. (Learn more about REAL in our book *The Dirt on Learning*.)

## *Relational*

When we say relational, we're referring to the relationship students form not only with Jesus and with the adults in the program but also with other students. We've found that student-to-student talk and interaction leads to greater understanding and learning. When kids talk and work together, they learn more, remember it longer, and apply it more readily.

Look at how Jesus grouped his followers. His disciples interacted together, growing closer to one another and to their Savior.

Kids work and worship in small disciple groups for these Ah-Ha experiences, also growing closer to one another and to their Savior.

## Experiential

Each of the Ah-Ha's described in these pages is experiential. Students will learn by doing.

God never intended worship to be a spectator sport. Worship is participatory. So each of these Ah-Ha's makes worship active, fully engaging each individual. Students will use their hands, eyes, ears, and other senses to explore the essence of God.

Research shows that people remember more when they're actively involved. Though we may remember less than 10 percent of what we read or what we hear from a speaker, we typically remember 90 percent of what we actively experience.

Jesus knew this during his earthly ministry. Look at the active lesson Jesus taught using foot-washing, for example. He could have preached a sermon about servant-hood. But in this case he knelt and washed his disciples' feet to make a powerful and memorable impact. Likewise these Ah-Ha's use experiences to make an impact.

We call these "Ah-Ha's" because participants experience "ah-ha" moments. Rather than merely being told what to believe, they discover God's truths embedded in the experiences. And because they make the discoveries themselves, the learning is more powerful, sticks longer, and crosses over more readily into life application.

## Applicable

The learning contained in these Ah-Ha's is designed to connect directly to kids' everyday lives. These aren't exercises in transferring information. Rather, they're experiences aimed at life transformation.

This is a new concept for many in the church. For decades, some have viewed the church's chief role as similar to that of a history class—the mere transfer of histori-cal facts. But somehow they've lost sight of the example Jesus gave to us. His min-istry was not constructed around fact drills but around building a relationship. His teachings weren't directed at warehousing information but at applying God's truths to people's lives right then and there. Jesus was, and is—in a word—*relevant*.

That's what we mean by applicable.

### Learner-based

These Ah-Ha experiences are designed for today's teenagers. But we know teenagers are not a homogenous group. They're each wired a little differently. So these experiences reflect a diverse variety of individual preferences and learning styles. Some kids will be attracted to certain choices, while some others will be drawn to other choices. That's being learner-based.

To contrast, a teacher-based approach is designed around the teacher's preferred style. "This is how I'm comfortable teaching," a teacher-based leader will say. To that we say this ministry isn't about you or what makes you comfortable. This ministry is about your students. It's the teacher's job to do what's necessary to adapt, mold, and reinvent one's self to help the students learn and grow in their relationship to the Lord.

A learner-based approach is concerned with learner results. In this case, that means the results of a deepened relationship with the Lord and an expression of that relationship through worship. The focus is on the learner. In contrast, a teacher-based approach is often more concerned with what the teacher does. Teacher-based proponents often fixate on how much content is sent. They'll prepare fact-heavy messages with little regard to how much of the transmitted information actually sticks.

These Ah-Ha's aren't concerned with how much information the teacher or leader dispatches into the air but how much long-lasting impact the experiences have on students' relationship with the Lord.

# STUDENT CHOICE

These experiences are designed to be offered to students on a menu of sorts. We advocate listing several of these options on a ballot each month or so. Give each student the opportunity to make a first, second, and third choice. Then tally the results and assign students to experiences according to their preferences. Based on the size of your group, run several Ah-Ha experiences simultaneously.

(SAMPLE BALLOT)

# Ballot for _____

Look over the choices for this month's worship experiences and mark your choices.
1 = first choice; 2 = second choice; 3 = third choice

⬜ **ON-THE-STREET DOUBTERS.** Here's your chance to be a part of a video news crew. You'll travel to nearby locations to interview people who'll tell you their doubts about God and the Bible.

⬜ **SILENT SINGERS.** You'll learn sign language to sing and share with the congregation.

⬜ **PRAYER WALL CONSTRUCTION TEAM.** You'll be "backstage" for this activity. You'll help build a prayer wall with lumber and nails and create a place for people to write their prayers.

**weblink Get Graphics & Ballot Blurbs Online!**

Designing your own ballots? Go to **www.grouppublishing.com/ creativefaithahhas/ballotextras** to download the illustrations used in this book as well as the ballot blurbs for all 45 Ah-Ha's.

Why give kids choices? They'll jump into their chosen experiences with more enthusiasm because they chose what to do. And when they have more enthusiasm, they'll enjoy the experience more, learn more, and grow more.

Think about yourself. Don't you find yourself learning more and remembering more when you're involved in something of your own choosing? You know a lot about your favorite hobby because you chose it. You would know less and display less passion if someone else had assigned a hobby to you.

And no one has to bribe you to pursue your chosen hobby. Church leaders too often try extrinsic motivators, such as prizes, to bribe kids into certain activities or behaviors. Frankly, we're more than a little uneasy about bribing people to deepen their relationship with Jesus. We would rather see students be more intrinsically motivated to get to know the Lord. Offering them choices allows them to follow their interests and their God-given gifts.

# ADULT INVOLVEMENT

These Ah-Ha's offer great opportunities for kids' parents to participate. All of these experiences require various amounts of adult help. We've had no trouble finding willing parent helpers and other adults.

As often indicated in our project descriptions, look for adults who may have a special interest in the type of project at hand. Ask a woodworking hobbyist to help with woodcrafts. Ask a drama type to help with dramas and puppet presentations. Ask an avid photographer to help with the photography projects.

Adults readily agree to help because the projects intersect with their interests—and it's short term, usually just a few weeks.

# CONGREGATION INVOLVEMENT

You'll notice that many of the experiences can be included in regular congregational worship services. Others are designed to culminate in a visual display in a prominent spot for the entire congregation to see.

This visibility adds significance and power to the experiences on several levels:

• Plugging these Ah-Ha's into the life of the church helps kids experience active church involvement that continues beyond the end of the program. They start a habit of active ministry that carries on into adulthood. They experience putting their faith into action.

• When your Ah-Ha work appears in front of the entire congregation, your kids receive concrete affirmation that they're a full-fledged part of the body of Christ. And we've found that student attendance in congregational worship increases when kids know their work will be on display.

• The fruits of these Ah-Ha's demonstrate to the congregation that your church includes and embraces young people. They and their work become visible. Your existing families *and* visiting families see that youth are important.

• These Ah-Ha's provide powerful and memorable additions to congregational worship. We've heard congregation members remark weeks and months later about the meaningful work the kids contributed to Sunday morning services.

# GET STARTED

Glance through the Ah-Ha's in the pages that follow. Get a feel for the type of experiences your young people can explore. Then form a planning team.

As we explained in the Introduction, you may wish to engage your planning team in forming a purpose statement. This will help guide your plans.

You may wish to involve your pastor at this point. If you're able to include the fruits of your Ah-Ha experiences in congregational worship, ask your pastor to explain upcoming sermon and worship themes. You can then choose Ah-Ha's that will support the upcoming emphases.

Feel free to adapt, expand, or shrink the Ah-Ha's. Make them your own. They'll work with all sizes of groups. If you have only three or four kids, fine! You already have a small group without needing to follow any instructions to "break into small groups." If you have three hundred kids, fine! Just use more small groups and offer more choices.

Ready? Set? Go! And engage your kids in unforgettable faith explorations!

## Design a "Thank You" Plan

Want to advocate youth ministry in your church? Teenagers can be invisible in a church. Here's an easy way to highlight their unique contributions:

Always keep a list of the names of the youth and adults who participate in these Creative Faith Ah-Ha's! Put their names in the church newsletter or bulletin. Plaster their names everywhere. The more you show the congregation that teenagers are important, the more you elevate the youth ministry. Showing respect for their contribution in the life of the church gives them honor and thanks.

And look at these additional benefits:

- Youth feel valued and want to continue plugging in.
- Adults feel valued and want to stay connected with young people.
- The entire church benefits from the fresh perspectives.

An easy way to do this is to assign someone the responsibility of giving credit after each project. Ask an organized, administrative type who'd love to contribute his or her talents in this way. Then be sure to thank that person!

# CREATiVE FAiTH

# AH-HA'S!

# ON-THE-STREET DOUBTERS

### Create a video that uncovers doubts people have about God and the Bible.

## BALLOT BLURB

Here's your chance to be a part of a news crew. You'll travel to nearby locations to interview and videotape people who'll tell you their doubts about God and the Bible.

## SCRIPTURELIFE CONNECTIONS

● Discuss how doubts and faith can coexist.

● Check out Jesus' encounter with his doubting disciple, Thomas, in John 20:24-31.

● Study Peter's water-walking attempt in Matthew 14:22-32; or mountain-moving faith in Matthew 21:21-22; or how to treat doubters in Jude 22.

## STAFF You'll Need

◯ Find a leader who has dreamed of being a reporter, who can help teenagers run video equipment and isn't afraid to coach the interviewing of people on the street—oh, and who isn't put off by someone saying, "No comment."

◯ Recruit drivers who are willing to navigate your "news vehicles." (Parents work great!)

## STUFF You'll Need

◯ video cameras, tapes, editing equipment

Arm small teams of teenagers with video cameras. Have each team load into one car, since groups larger than a carload might scare off interviewees. Choose locations where unsuspecting passersby might be willing to chat briefly. Mall parking lots work well.

Assign outgoing kids to be "reporters," and have the rest of each group be the camera crew. Prepare a brief introduction and list of questions. Try this: **"Hi. I'm _____, and we're doing a video project for our youth group. I have just a couple questions. OK?"** (If shoppers are in a hurry, they can politely decline, but we found most people curious and willing to oblige.)

Continue with questions like these:

• **Many people find things about God and the Bible hard to believe. What do you find hard to believe?**

• **What part of the Bible seems more like fiction than fact?**

Thank the interviewees for participating. Bring along a few brochures from your church, and invite interviewees to the worship service premiering the video.

Set up a time to review all the interviews, especially if you have multiple news crews. (Hey, you have an excuse for a get-together!) Select brief clips. Save the most amusing for the first and last impression. Show the video to add spark to the pastor's Sunday morning sermon.

## Our Own "AH-HA's" :-)

Surprisingly, people were cooperative and willing to share their doubts. Maybe they were most amazed that a church would be open to their God questions. And they do have questions!

Not only did we give doubters airtime but we also met people who told us about their strong belief in God and the Bible. Either encounter gave students permission to raise their own doubts or confirm their own faith convictions.

We even had interviewees who were looking for a church home. No doubt about it—our project turned into an outreach tool!

## "UH-OH's"

(Mistakes we made, so you don't have to.)

We tried interviewing in supermarket parking lots. Some patrons complained to store personnel—and we got shooed away by the manager. (Our kids thought "getting busted" was the highlight of the day.) Public sidewalks and mall parking lots work better.

**weblink** Get Graphics & Ballot Blurbs **Online!**

Designing your own ballots? Go to **www.grouppublishing.com/ creativefaithahhas/ballotextras** to download the illustrations used in this book as well as the ballot blurbs for all 45 Ah-Ha's.

# BE INSTRUMENTAL

Express your God-given musical talents by instrumentally accompanying your congregation's singing.

## BALLOT BLURB

☐ If you play an instrument—any instrument—we need you to make music for our church band or orchestra. Depending on what you play, we'll compose a special accompaniment for our congregation to showcase your God-given musical talents.

## SCRIPTURELIFE CONNECTIONS

● Celebrate the unique body of talents in your church by reading 1 Corinthians 12:12-27.

● Praise God for the musicians in your church and shout Psalm 150.

### STAFF You'll Need

○ Make a note of music lovers. For example, middle school, junior high, or high school band directors can compose music for instruments that match teenagers' playing capabilities. (Don't frustrate kids with music that's too difficult.) Or enlist a music enthusiast who knows computer music composition programs to create the accompaniment. If your church has a music minister, here's a great way to connect that person with youth.

### STUFF You'll Need

○ music scores customized for your unique selection of instruments

○ other music accompaniment, if needed

# MAKING IT HAPPEN

Find out which instruments students play. Next, enlist your music leader to write or transpose straight accompaniment or descants for song selections. Choose songs that highlight the instruments represented; then customize the accompaniment to your instrumental assortment. Use songs that the congregation can sing. If practice time permits, add music for before or after church or during the offering.

Let your congregation know what you're up to. Your budding musicians might not resemble the Boston Philharmonic, but parents and churchgoers will delight in young people sounding off this way!

## "UH-OH's" :-O
(Mistakes we made, so you don't have to.)

Make sure to plan for extra practices, if necessary. Some kids (and parents) get pretty worried if they don't feel confident.

## Our Own "AH-HA's" :-)

One Sunday, a nervous mom sat beside us. "Josh can't play that well," she confided. To her surprise, Josh played his solo trumpet descant without a hitch. She beamed with pride—and God was praised!

Every time we've done this, we're amazed at the musical talent (and unique assortment) that surfaces. OK, it can be a bit unusual to find what works for a band consisting of a French horn, snare drum, clarinet, and tuba! Students get to see that their extracurricular music activities do have a place in the church. Plus, they get to work together to make a joyful noise to the Lord.

Guess what? This project became an entry point for the local public school band director to link to our church.

# AH-HA 3 — KEEPSAKE CREATIONS

Design a special scrapbook as a gift to celebrate another student's faith commitment.

Become part of a group to prepare a special keepsake for students confirming their faith. Shh...it'll be a surprise!

## SCRIPTURELIFE CONNECTIONS

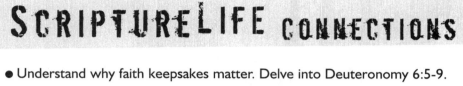

- Understand why faith keepsakes matter. Delve into Deuteronomy 6:5-9.

- Study and speculate on what it was like for Jesus' growing-up years in Luke 2:40.

- Make commitments to grow in faith. Use Colossians 3:12-17 as a foundation.

## STAFF You'll Need

○ Look for scrapbook enthusiasts, particularly moms of teenagers. They'll love this kind of project!

## STUFF You'll Need

- ○ small scrapbook per student
- ○ scrapbooking tools to share
- ○ "Faith" letters from each student's family and friends
- ○ photos of each student
- ○ favorite Bible verse chosen by each student
- ○ markers, stickers

# MAKING IT HAPPEN

This project takes some extra work. But trust us: It's worth the time and effort!

Have a team of students divvy up the names and phone numbers of the gift recipients' parents. Legwork involves calling recipients' parents to have them secretly write a "faith" letter to their son or daughter, commenting on why a time of faith commitment is so important. Not only ask parents to write notes but also ask grandparents, godparents, or other significant people who've played a part in helping nurture that teenager's faith. Include the youth minister, small group leader, or Sunday school teachers. (Each small group leader at our church contributed a special message or prayer.)

While asking for letters, also collect special photos. They might include pictures of the recipient's baptism, youth retreats, service projects, family events, sports, or other interests—any photos that express what's special to the recipient.

Give parents the details on where to send or deposit the letters and photos. Make sure they know the deadline. Then swear them to secrecy.

Find out each student's favorite Bible verse. How about asking a calligraphy enthusiast to artistically write out each verse by hand? Or use a cool computer font to do the work for you.

Gather keepsake creations for a fun time of scrapbooking. Make sure you have all the necessary supplies—the scrapbook itself, markers, stickers, the letters from family members and friends, favorite Bible verses, and photos. (By the way, our church covered the costs as a gift to each student.) You may want to save spaces for adding photos taken during the special day.

Wrap each personalized scrapbook treasure. Then plan how you'll ceremoniously give it to each person. It'll be something the recipient will cherish for a lifetime.

## Our Own "AH-HA's" :-)

We used the scrapbook as a confirmation memento for the students' special day. We began each keepsake scrapbook with the Bible verse each student had chosen.

Students' family members were truly moved by the personalized gifts. The touching and fun letters from family members and friends brought laughter and tears. The letters gave an avenue for expressing heartfelt love and faith that people often find hard to say out loud.

One grandfather chronicled the joy he felt when Andrew was born, what he saw in Andrew as he grew up, and why Andrew's new step of faith was so important to him. Not long after that, Andrew's grandpa passed away. That scrapbook has become an extra-special treasure.

# IN THE SPOTLIGHT

Hint: Consider using Ah-Ha's 6 (p. 26) and 7 (p. 28) alongside this one.

Demonstrate a biblical point
through drama.

## BALLOT BLURB

☐ Here's your chance to let your acting talents shine. Put your dramatic abilities to good use and perform for church.

## SCRIPTURE LIFE CONNECTIONS

● Unlimited. Depending on the drama you choose, pray for guidance as you act out the scriptural points you will teach. (Most Christian drama resources give Bible references that undergird the script. So your job is easy.)

## STAFF You'll Need

◯ Recruit a patient drama-type person who enjoys coaching teenagers.

## STUFF You'll Need

◯ Any Group skit book is specifically designed to be easy and to-the-point. They don't require Hollywood caliber actors to pull them off. Try these (available at www.grouppublishing.com):

● *Ultimate Skits: 20 Parables for Driving Home Your Point*
● *Hilarious Skits for Youth Ministry*
● *Goof-Proof Skits for Youth Ministry*
● *Goof-Proof Skits for Youth Ministry 2*

◯ Collect the necessary props. Or check out Ah-Ha 7 (p. 28) to pair with your efforts. (It's listed as "Puppet Players Support Team" but could work for drama, too.)

Compile a few skit book resources. (See the "Staff and Stuff" box for ideas.) Find out what theme or Bible passage the pastor will be using in worship. Let teenagers sift through the books together to find dramas that reinforce the pastor's message. Half the fun is reading through the scripts! And besides, it's good practice for spotting the real hams in your midst.

Practice your dramatic production, and present it for the whole congregation to enjoy.

## Our Own "AH-HA's" :-)

If your teenagers are like ours, you might see shy, reserved students explode with talent. We were surprised at how committed they were to memorizing sketches to do their best. They were willing to put in extra time to prepare. And they soaked up the compliments!

## "UH-OH's"
(Mistakes we made, so you don't have to.)

Don't make the mistake we did when we began using youth in drama. Beware of inadequate sound. Sometimes the congregation couldn't hear because we hadn't practiced enough with the microphones. Oops!

# MUSIC MAKERS

## Sing to the Lord!

**Hint:** If you want, you can combine this with "Silent Singers," Ah-Ha 9 (p. 32).

**BALLOT BLURB**

☐ You'll make a joyful noise to the Lord while helping lead worshippers in song.

## SCRIPTURELIFE CONNECTIONS

● Grab a concordance and find all the references to *sing* and *singing*. (Don't confuse your Bible study with a typo, *sin* and *sinning*, instead of *sing* and *singing*. That happened to us once! Oops!)

### STAFF You'll Need

◯ Corral a person who loves to sing and hear teenagers praising the Lord in song. Don't overlook a teenager or young adult who loves music.

◯ If you want live accompaniment, arrange for that, too.

### STUFF You'll Need

◯ music songbooks and CDs

◯ lyrics for all

◯ music accompaniment (Decide if it'll be live or recorded.)

# MAKING IT HAPPEN

Bring together students who love to sing. Provide songbooks and CDs and have an accompanist on hand. Select songs that fit your worship theme. Or have teenagers choose favorite songs to sing before, during, or after the service. How about singing a song as their offering?

## Our Own "AH-HA's" :-)

Most often girls signed up for this one at our church. We discovered girls who were great at harmonizing. They really sounded good!

We're not sure if the guys' voices were changing and they were self-conscious, but this choice wasn't as popular with them.

We learned that we got more accomplished during practice if the songs were prese- 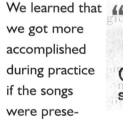 lected. One time we spent so much time thumbing through songbooks that we failed to put together any songs we felt comfortable sharing with the congregation.

## "UH-OH's"
(Mistakes **we** made, so you don't have to.)

**weblink** Get Graphics & Ballot Blurbs **Online!**
Designing your own ballots? Go to **www.grouppublishing.com/ creativefaithahhas/ballotextras** to download the illustrations used in this book as well as the ballot blurbs for all 45 Ah-Ha's.

# PUPPET PLAYERS

You can share God's message—even if you're hiding behind a stage!

**Hint:** This Ah-Ha works great with Ah-Ha's 4 (p. 22) and 7 (p. 28).

## BALLOT BLURB

☐ Lend a hand to perform a puppet play for a children's message in church.

## SCRIPTURELIFE CONNECTIONS

● Unlimited. Once you've chosen the Bible story or point you want to make, use the puppet skit resources to provide the Scripture and message to pray about and study in preparation.

### STAFF You'll Need

○ Ask for a helping hand from someone who is "puppet positive." Drama-types love this.

### STUFF You'll Need

○ Check out an array of instant puppet resources from Group. They're easy and lots of fun. Many come complete with CDs filled with voices, background music, and fun sound effects. Try these resources (available at www.grouppublishing.com):

- *Instant Puppet Skits: 20 Stories From People Who Met Jesus*
- *Just Add Puppets: 20 Instant Puppet Skits for Children's Ministry*
- *Instant Skits for Children's Ministry*

Scope out favorite puppet plays from the vast resources you've collected. (You did get those vast resources, didn't you?) Group Publishing offers fun and easy ones with CDs that simplify sound requirements.

If you don't use a prerecorded script, decide if you'll have puppeteers speak their lines (loudly and clearly) or prerecord your own version.

Have fun practicing the scripts as you enact them with puppets. Get ready to present them to your audience with flair!

## Our Own "AH-HA's" :-)

We've done both live and prerecorded scripts. Each has its advantages. The spoken ones allow teenagers to flex their dramatic muscles. On the other hand, if time, ease, and assured clarity for the audience are important to you, pop in an instant puppet script CD. It's loads of fun and still allows teenagers lots of participation.

## "UH-OH's"
(Mistakes we made, so you don't have to.)

Be careful that the puppeteers aren't having such a good time that they forget that an audience is watching. We've had puppeteers get the giggles and forget what they were doing, and, well, the audience lost some of the meaning. The kids sure had fun, though.

# PUPPET PLAYERS SUPPORT TEAM

### Expressing faith can happen "behind the scenes" too!

**Hint:** Consider combining forces with "Puppet Players," Ah-Ha 6 (p. 26).

## BALLOT BLURB

☐ You'll be back-stage helpers for props and sound. You'll help make our Puppet Players look and sound good.

## SCRIPTURE LIFE CONNECTIONS

● Follow the lead of the Puppet Players (p. 26). Join the Puppet Players for prayer and Bible study highlights dependent on the script you choose.

## STAFF You'll Need

◯ **Pinpoint an organized adult who likes to work behind the scenes. This person will help the support team organize for their mission and become familiar with the Puppet Players' needs.**

## STUFF You'll Need

◯ **This depends on the script chosen. You'll need to work closely with the Puppet Players.**

# MAKING IT HAPPEN

Here's the place for kids who detest the spotlight. Plus, it's a real way to experience servant leadership.

Get a copy of the Puppet Players' script. Brainstorm as a Puppet Players Support Team how to build a puppet stage (if necessary). Figure out what props and sound effects you need. Then divvy up who will collect what. (Just think, "We're the people the Puppet Players need to perfect their performance." Say that five times!)

Decide who will do what as the "stage hands," distribute props, and run sound (if needed).

Our Own "AH-HA's" :-)

We remember most how Kate, a caring, soft-spoken mom, worked with a small team of shy, quiet guys. They did a great job and came up with hilarious props and sound effects to make the Puppet Players a success!

# PUPPET CREATORS

Design puppet characters to support the Puppet Players.

**Hint:** If you want, combine this with Ah-Ha's 6 (p. 26) and 7 (p. 28) for a real team effort!

## BALLOT BLURB

☐ Get in on the act by creating puppet characters for an awesome puppet play.

## SCRIPTURELIFE CONNECTIONS

● Unlimited. Find out what script and Scripture the Puppet Players plan to use. Then study and pray about the theme you've chosen.

● Do this all as a combo, and celebrate the use of teamwork for God's purposes.

## STAFF You'll Need

○ Be on the prowl for an artistic, imaginative type who loves to watch kids' creativity.

## STUFF You'll Need

○ Go on a shopping spree at your local craft store. Pick up a variety of goodies such as Styrofoam balls (they make great heads), dowels (super for various body parts and skeletal systems), big wiggly eyes (what else?), felt and cloth scraps (perfect for wardrobes), yarn and fake fur (a wig-maker's dream), hot glue guns, and other surprise stuff.

## MAKING IT HAPPEN

Stock up on "crafty" materials that will naturally unleash kids' creativity. Check out the "Stuff" section on page 30. You get the idea.

Familiarize your Puppet Creators with the puppet script and characters needed. Then let them loose!

## Our Own "AH-HA's" :-)

We purposely haven't given too many specifics here, just to let you experience kid-creativity. And it'll come from girls and guys alike!

Here's a favorite memory from this experience: We watched students include Brandon in their puppet-making decisions. You see, their peer Brandon is confined to a wheelchair, unable to speak or move normally, but filled with a love for the Lord and his classmates.

We watched with lumps in our throats as kids asked Brandon which color yarn to use for the puppets' hair. By offering a choice to Brandon, he could use his eye movement to point to his selection. Ministry times like these prove that the result of a project isn't necessarily the goal—it's God using young people working together, including each other, and experiencing the body of Christ.

# SILENT SINGERS

Show people music with
sign language.

**Hint:** If you want, you can combine this with "Music Makers," Ah-Ha 5 (p. 24).

## BALLOT BLURB

☐ You'll learn sign language to sing and share with the congregation.

## SCRIPTURELIFE CONNECTIONS

● Using the song(s) you've chosen, look up the corresponding Scripture themes. Point out how Scripture might have inspired the words and how your signing will inspire deeper understanding of those words.

● Do a Scripture study of Jesus' healing a deaf man. See Mark 7:31-37. How can we use our weaknesses to bring God glory?

## STAFF You'll Need

◯ If you're fortunate, you may know someone who's hearing impaired who could help. Otherwise, find someone who has an interest in learning sign language.

## STUFF You'll Need

◯ CD or music with lyrics

◯ sign language information. Check out these Web sites for general help. You may be able to find sign language for particular songs by doing a search on the Internet.

● http://www.apocalypsefoundation.co.za/HTML/Deaf3.htm
● http://commtechlab.msu.edu/sites/aslweb/

# MAKING IT HAPPEN

Select a simple song. (The chorus of "Awesome God" works great!) Any praise song or song about Jesus makes for great sign-language "picture songs." For example, the sign for *Jesus* is shown by pointing to the nail wound in each hand, one hand at a time.

Either sing along or sign with a CD or choir. Have students stand up front so everyone can see their hands. They may even want to dress alike to create a visual image of "one body" moving together as a silent choir.

Our church is blessed to have Elizabeth, a teacher/principal, who is hearing impaired. She worked with the students to teach sign language in worship.

Your church may not have an Elizabeth, but you may be surprised how many people have an interest in sign language. Or how teenagers may take up the challenge to learn sign language. Don't limit this just to teenagers. Include children and adults too.

Who knows? This could be the start of a special ministry at your church to the hearing impaired.

# PHENOMENAL PHOTOGRAPHERS

AH-HA 10

### Photograph what you're thankful for.

☐ You'll create a special Thanksgiving message in pictures to use in a worship prayer.

## SCRIPTURELIFE CONNECTIONS

● Luke 17:11-19 recounts a poignant story of thanksgiving, or lack thereof. Have teenagers take a hard look at these words and tell with whom they most identify.

● Visit the book of Psalms to help create a thank you prayer. You can start with Psalm 95:1-7 and 100:1-5.

● Use this project as a launching pad for a series on prayer or thankfulness.

## STAFF You'll Need

○ **Calling all photo buffs!** Listen for adults who make photography a hobby and a passion.

## STUFF You'll Need

○ cameras, slide film, projector; or digital camera and appropriate equipment

# MAKING IT HAPPEN

This Ah-Ha takes Thanksgiving to another level. Encourage a small group of photographers to list things for which they're thankful. The next time you meet, pile into a car and go on a "Thanksgiving hunt."

Have the Thanksgiving hunters photograph personal thanksgivings as well as community-related pictures.

Choose an instrumental song or a favorite Thanksgiving song for background music. Create a slide show or PowerPoint presentation with the photos put to music. If you have the technology available, digital cameras make it extra easy to incorporate your work into PowerPoint or MediaShout.

 Get Graphics & Ballot Blurbs **Online!**

Designing your own ballots? Go to **www.grouppublishing.com/ creativefaithahhas/ballotextras** to download the illustrations used in this book as well as the ballot blurbs for all 45 Ah-Ha's.

 Our Own "AH-HA's" :-)

Our adult volunteer's favorite hobby was taking and developing pictures. Not only did he complete the Thanksgiving prayer project with the teenagers but he also invited them to his home to learn how to develop pictures.

The Thanksgiving picture prayer meant so much to our congregation because kids took shots of recognizable local areas. That added a real, personalized touch. Many shots highlighted the beautiful mountains. The prayer made us extra thankful to live at the base of the majestic Rocky Mountains, one of God's creative masterpieces.

# RESEARCH SPECIALISTS

Interview community residents by telephone to learn what they believe about prayer.

**BALLOT BLURB**

☐ You'll conduct a telephone poll of citizens to ask if they believe that God answers prayer.

## SCRIPTURELIFE CONNECTIONS

● Delve into Scripture that focuses on prayer. Study Matthew 6:5-13 (the Lord's Prayer); Mark 11:22-25 (faith and power in prayer); 1 Thessalonians 5:17 (pray continually); and James 5:13-16 (pray in faith).

● Investigate people in the Bible who prayed and talked with God. Discuss how God answered their prayers. For example, Abraham pleading for Sodom and Gomorrah (Genesis 18:20-33); Moses and the burning bush (Exodus 3:15); Jonah in the big fish (Jonah 2:1-10); Jesus in the Garden of Gethsemane (Luke 22:39-46); Paul and Silas in jail (Acts 16:22-26).

## STAFF You'll Need

○ Enlist someone who likes phone research and organizing.

## STUFF You'll Need

○ access to telephones and cell phones

○ local phone directory

○ paper and pens to record and tally results

Creative Faith Ah-Ha's

36

# MAKING IT HAPPEN

See if you can take over the church office. Multiple phones would be great. Get permission for kids to use their cell phones. And you're ready for business!

Gather students willing to make random phone-call surveys and work together to set up your own "tele-survey" system. Decide random phone numbers to call. For instance, have students call the third name in the left-hand column on each page of the phone book to result in a random survey.

Create a "script." For example: **"Hi, my name is ___, and I'm doing a research project for my church youth group. I have a couple questions that will take about two minutes, OK? Do you believe that God answers prayer? Why do you feel that way?"**

Have teenagers record on paper the answers to every question. Then tally the results and hand them over to your pastor to include in an upcoming sermon. You might want to make a poster displaying the survey results for people to see as they come into worship. That's what we did.

**Our Own "AH-HA's" :-)**

This is the idea we thought no one would choose. Were we surprised! But then again, maybe not. We forgot that teenagers love to talk on the phone. One after the other dialed, listened, and recorded surveys. Even when people hung up on them (rejection!), they didn't seem to mind! They were on a mission.

Not only was compiling the information interesting, but it also intrigued congregation members to hear local survey results reported in Sunday's sermon.

**"UH-OH's"**
(Mistakes we made, so you don't have to.)

Looking back, we could have used the phone calls as a great object lesson for prayer. We could've pointed out how God is always "on the line, ready to receive our 'calls' "—God is ready to listen. Anytime. Anywhere.

# AH-HA 12

# FOTO FUN PRAYER

Use photographs to
portray psalms.

☐ Try out your pho-
tography talents to
create a special "pic-
ture prayer." If you
like the visual arts
and showing God's love
with a camera, this
one's for you.

## SCRIPTURELIFE CONNECTIONS

● Choose favorite psalms as in-depth prayer studies. Here's a starter list:
Psalms 8; 18:1-19; 33; 51:1-17; 139; 150.

## STAFF You'll Need

◯ Grab a teen-friendly photo buff, someone who loves
looking at the world through a lens.

## STUFF You'll Need

◯ Bibles

◯ cameras, slide film, or digital media

◯ slides, computer/projector

◯ music (optional)

# MAKING IT HAPPEN

Picture this: A group of teenagers digging into a favorite psalm to create a picture of prayer. Start with Scripture. Then have kids choose how to portray a favorite passage visually. Psalms work great because they convey emotion and pictures. Try any of these:

- Psalm 8 (the majesty of God's creation)
- Psalm 18:1-19 (God is our rock and rescues us)
- Psalm 33 (joyful praise)
- Psalm 51:1-17 (forgiveness)
- Psalm 139 (God knows everything)
- Psalm 150 (musical praise)

Arm every person with a camera and film for optimum involvement. Or go digital. The goal is to capture images that express God's Word.

Have kids "edit" all their photos by choosing the ones that best portray Scripture and good quality photography. Create a "big screen" show—for your whole church, if possible.

For added impact, play background music as a team of teen readers reads Scripture passages while their photography appears.

Our Own "AH-HA's" :-)

Not only did this experience tap into teenagers' photography skills, but the pictures also made a strong connection to prayer and Scripture. The students read the psalm that matched with each photo as prayers during a special worship service for the entire church. It was very powerful and meaningful. This experience also helped demonstrate how relevant the psalms are to our lives as people of all ages watched God's Word depicted in pictures of places we all recognized.

# PHOTO GALLERY OF GOD'S PEOPLE IN ACTION

### Take pictures of church activities, and post them for all to see.

☐ Be a spy with a camera's eye! Capture on film what happens at church. Then create a photo gallery of God's people in action.

## SCRIPTURELIFE CONNECTIONS

● Do a church checkup. Read Matthew 16:13-19 ("On this rock I will build my church"); 1 Corinthians 12:4-27 (the body of Christ); Colossians 1:24-27 (the mystery, which is Christ in you).

## STAFF You'll Need

◯ Look for someone who loves to take pictures and enjoys working with teenagers.

## STUFF You'll Need

◯ Bibles
◯ cameras, film

Once you have your fleet (large or small) of photojournalists, choose a time at your church that reflects lots of activity. It could be a Sunday morning, or maybe it's a Wednesday night when there is a flurry of groups meeting. Encourage students to look for people doing ministry around the church and to take pictures of "the church in action."

We found Wednesday nights to be the best "happening time" for all ages: junior high classes, midweek family meal, choirs, children's groups, youth group. (We also did this with drivers who buzzed around the community to capture familiar faces and places.)

Develop all the film, and come together to create a poster board display attached to a wooden frame. (See "Prayer Wall Construction Team," Ah-Ha 14 [p. 42], for the frame idea. It's just one more way to involve others.)

We watched congregation members pause, reflect, and smile as they soaked up a teenager's view of their church.

# PRAYER WALL CONSTRUCTION TEAM

### Build a prayer wall.

## SCRIPTURELIFE CONNECTIONS

● Ask. Seek. Knock. Take time to dig into Matthew 7:7-8. Invite teenagers to tell about times God answered their prayers.

● Add Matthew 7:9-11. Wrestle with understanding God's wisdom in answering our prayers like a dad would answer a child's requests.

## STAFF You'll Need

◯ Locate an eager construction worker. (Just think, Jesus was a carpenter who might have signed up for this one. Wasn't this his specialty?)

## STUFF You'll Need

◯ lumber, nails, saw, hammers, measuring tape

◯ poster board or newsprint

◯ string or yarn

◯ masking tape

◯ markers or pens

You'll want your prayer wall to become a special centerpiece for worshippers as they arrive, so you'll want to choose a prominent spot in the church's entrance area. Make sure people can write prayers on all sides.

Challenge teenagers to build a freestanding wooden frame to cover and "dress" in newsprint or poster board. Five to six feet high works well. Be certain the wall withstands pressure from writers working on both sides at once. Attach multiple markers with yarn or string for passersby to jot their prayer requests.

Design an attractive headline: "Prayer Wall: Please add your prayer requests so we can pray for you."

Model how that's done by inviting all the prayer wall construction workers to start the praying by writing their own prayers on the wall.

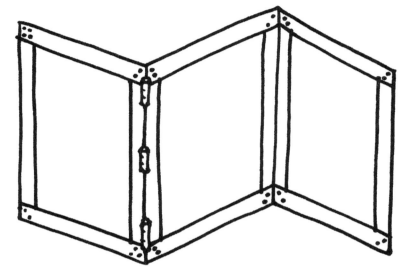

## Our Own "AH-HA's" :-)

We watched a powerful prayer community unfold on Sunday mornings. The prayer wall evolved into a visual collection of handwriting that revealed the family of God. It showed deliberately scrawled handwriting from frail elderly hands, surrounded by elementary and preschool printing, teen "bubble letters," and artwork. We saw all ages coming to God, coming together for prayer support.

I still remember the mental memory "snapshot" of a small child on her knees carefully writing her prayer, a teenager nearby doing the same, next to a grandma also writing her prayer.

## "UH-OH's"
### (Mistakes we made, so you don't have to.)

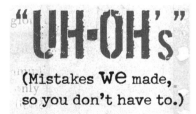

Thinking back, we should have taken time with the students to gather around the prayer wall. As a group, we could have knelt around the wall and lifted up the congregation's prayer concerns together. That would underscore the value of this project even more.

# THANKSGIVING PRAYER CHAIN

Surround your worship area with words of thanks on a paper chain.

BALLOT BLURB

☐ You'll cut and craft a beautiful prayer chain that will represent the prayers of our worshippers.

## SCRIPTURELIFE CONNECTIONS

● Take a closer look at Paul's prayer in Philippians. As a team, read (and pray) Philippians 1:3-11. Talk about how these words might be said of your church.

● Put verses 9-11 into your own prayer words for your local congregation. For the fun of it, point out the reference to "chains" in verse 7 and how that connects with the prayer chain you're about to create!

## STAFF You'll Need

◯ Appoint one of your church's "prayer warriors" to join in on this, along with someone "crafty." This is such an easy project to lead; you may want to find a parent who'll give it a whirl with the kids.

## STUFF You'll Need

◯ colored construction paper

◯ scissors

◯ stapler and staples

◯ masking tape

# MAKING IT HAPPEN

Here's to resurrecting a fun and easy childhood project that can involve everybody.

For starters, cut 1-inch strips of colored construction paper. Decide if you want a rainbow of colors or thematic colors. For example, orange, yellow, and brown work great for fall or Thanksgiving; red and green go with Christmas. You get the idea.

Have teenagers hand out strips of paper to worshippers, inviting people to write what they're thankful for on the colored paper. (Or suggest another type of prayer, if you wish.) Collect all the paper prayers during the offering.

Set a time for teenagers to work as a "chain gang" to staple each prayer strip into a circle that connects with other circles to create a chain. Have them read and pray as the chain grows.

Hang the prayer chain so it encircles your worship area. Let it surround you with thanksgiving.

## Our Own "AH-HA's" :-)

Hundreds of people added to the chain. All ages participated, so it turned into a family-friendly prayer that surrounded us for a number of weeks. It portrayed not only our thankfulness but also how God's goodness surrounds us.

# AH-HA 16 GROWING GLOBE SURPRISE

### Design an intriguing sculpture that grows each week.

**BALLOT BLURB**

☐ Get ready to design a growing sculpture showing that God has the whole world in his hands.

## SCRIPTURELIFE CONNECTIONS

● Imagine Psalm 46 appearing in sculpture form. Sing "He's Got the Whole World in His Hands."

● Read Psalm 46 verse by verse, stopping after each verse to discuss how that verse looks, sounds, feels, and smells. Now you're ready to launch into creating a sculpture of God's hands holding the earth.

## STAFF You'll Need

◯ Find an artsy-craftsy type. If possible, bring in someone who knows sculpture—or at least papier-mâché.

## STUFF You'll Need

◯ wood, hammer, nails, and saw for the base

◯ chicken wire or other shapeable material to create a foundation for the papier-mâché

◯ papier-mâché paste: Combine ½ cup flour with 2 cups of cold water. Add this mixture to 2 cups boiling water in a pan, and bring it to a boil again. Remove the mix from the heat, and stir in 3 tablespoons of sugar. Once it cools, it's ready to use.

◯ strips of newspaper for the papier-mâché

◯ tempera paint, paintbrushes, and pans

# MAKING IT HAPPEN

This is a good four-week project, if you keep things moving.

Have your sculptors make plans in advance for a papier-mâché sculpture that can be assembled in sections to create a mystery for worshippers: "What is that? What are they making now?"

We wanted to say, "In His Hands," so each week one more phase of the sculpture appeared in the entryway to worship. It went something like this, so here's what can inspire you:

**Week 1**—Create a wooden base and a large pair of papier-mâché hands. Add a sign to clue people in on your project. Use your own ingenuity, or try something like " 'Work in Progress!' Signed: Your Church's Youth."

**Week 2**—Paint the hands. Then add a giant ball to be your globe. Cover the ball with papier-mâché as well. (The "whole world in his hands," get it?)

**Week 3**—Paint the globe blue. (Keep the sign up.)

**Week 4**—Paint the globe with green continents. Add a new sign: "In His Hands."

With a little imagination and a lot of papier-mâché, you can come up with your own ideas that create a sculpture message "in progress."

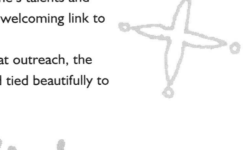

**Our Own "AH-HA's" :-)**

Loveland, Colorado, happens to be the home of many bronze sculptures and their sculptors. (Loveland hosts one of the world's largest sculpture shows each summer.) Our artistic adult leader partnered with a local sculptor (not a member of our church) to help lead the teenagers. This made the project an outreach honoring someone's talents and gifts. Plus, it became a welcoming link to our church.

In addition to a great outreach, the project built anticipation each week and tied beautifully to our pastor's sermon series.

# AH-HA 17 MAKE HEADLINES

Teenagers interview, write, and publish congregation members' faith stories.

**BALLOT BLURB**

☐ Become a reporter/writer/editor! You'll interview "famous" members of our congregation, write their faith stories, and publish them to share with the church family.

## SCRIPTURELIFE CONNECTIONS

● Take a look at 2 Corinthians 3:2-3. It describes Christians as "living letters" communicating Jesus.

● Talk about how everyone who believes in Jesus sees his or her as a testimony to his love. By putting these "living letters" into print, you'll help others see Jesus more clearly.

## STAFF You'll Need

◯ Enlist someone who enjoys writing and editing. Perhaps an English teacher, newspaper editor, journalist, or publisher would volunteer.

## STUFF You'll Need

◯ paper, pens, and clipboards (just to make it official!)

◯ tape recorder (optional)

◯ computer clip art (optional)

# MAKING IT HAPPEN

People love stories, especially real-life stories of people they know who have seen God at work in their lives. Interviewing people from your church is a great way to see God in action.

Plan to have "reporters" on deck during peak times church members gather: Sunday fellowship time over coffee and doughnuts, midweek activities, and right after church.

Send out your fleet of reporters, armed with pens and clipboards loaded with paper. Or turn on a tape recorder if your kids feel "scribe challenged."

Use a prepared list of interview questions to prompt people to tell students how God has worked in their lives. Try interview questions like these:

- **What is your name?**
- **How long have you been coming to our church? How did you learn about our church?**
- **When has God worked in a powerful way in your life?**
- **When has it been hard for you to believe in God? Why?**
- **When have you seen God answer your prayers?**
- **What would you tell someone who didn't believe in Jesus?**

Collect all the faith stories and edit them. That means deleting extraneous ideas that don't directly point to God at work in their lives. Condense what people said into brief, interesting stories.

Then make handouts that feature the stories. Use clip art. Or if you can, you may want to show a picture of the people you interviewed.

## Our Own "AH-HA's" :-)

We learned how open people can be in sharing their real struggles, hurts, and joys. Each Sunday morning gave us an opportunity to read how God touched people in our midst.

Hearing how real people share real faith was great not only for our young people but also for the rest of the congregation!

## "UH-OH's" (Mistakes we made, so you don't have to.)

If we were to do this again, we would suggest putting the stories in the church newsletter. Mailing to the entire congregation would've given the stories a wider distribution. Everyone could've read them—not just the people who attended one particular Sunday.

# AH-HA 18 ARTISTS' CORNER

Draw or paint artistic expressions of Jesus' journey to the cross.

*PAINT*

## SCRIPTURELIFE CONNECTIONS

- Survey the Gospels—Matthew, Mark, Luke, and John. Compare how each writer portrayed the week leading up to Jesus' death on the cross. (Note how Matthew is used on the following page.)

- Try this: Have the students take one week and draw their spiritual journey for that week. Use their drawings as a springboard for discussion and prayer. Compare their week to Jesus' final week leading up to his sacrifice on the cross.

## STAFF You'll Need

○ Look for an artist, an art teacher, or a master doodler.

## STUFF You'll Need

○ art supplies with plenty of paper. Assemble an array of artistic "tools": pens, pencils, colored pencils, markers, tempera paints, paintbrushes.

○ samples of Christian art to spark ideas (optional). For example, check out www.abba-art.com and other Christian art galleries on the Internet.

# MAKING IT HAPPEN

Pull together students who love to draw, doodle, and design. Provide picture "prompts" of Christian art and symbols. Then go straight to Scripture and focus on Jesus' week before his death.

Challenge artists to experiment with different creative approaches—pencil, colored pencil, markers, water colors, tempera paints, whatever.

Create a series of visual images of Jesus' journey to the cross. Dig into the Bible, and illustrate the following passages literally or figuratively:

• The Lord's Supper (Matthew 26:17-30): bread, cup, wheat, grapes

• The Garden of Gethsemane (Matthew 26:36-46): praying hands, garden nighttime scene

• Jesus' arrest (Matthew 26:47-56): swords, clubs, crowd, kiss

• Jesus before the Sanhedrin (Matthew 26:57-68): guards, priests, fists, violence

• Peter disowns Jesus (Matthew 26:31-35, 69-75): rooster, tears

• Judas hands himself over (Matthew 27:1-10): thirty silver coins, noose

• Jesus before Pilate (Matthew 27:11-26): water, basin

• Soldiers mock Jesus (Matthew 27:27-31): soldiers, robe, crown of thorns, king's staff

• The Crucifixion (Matthew 27:32-50): three crosses, a sign that says, "This is Jesus, King of the Jews."

Use this as a time of Bible study and prayer to discuss Jesus' personal sacrifice for each person.

When the art is ready, display it in a prominent place. (See Ah-Ha 20, "Calling All Carpenters" [p. 54], for display ideas.)

## Our Own "AH-HA's" :-)

You may be as amazed as we were at the tremendous talent exhibited. One budding artist, Alexi, loved to sketch, anytime, anywhere. So this Ah-Ha was a perfect way for her to express her faith. And she did a beautiful job with pencil drawings.

# AH-HA 19 SPY CAM

Capture a "tempting" situation on video.

☐ Use a video camera to collect candid camera shots for the pastor's sermon on temptation.

## SCRIPTURELIFE CONNECTIONS

● Dive into Jesus' encounter with the devil in Matthew 4:1-11. Analyze each tempting situation, and put it into a modern day context. What would the devil use today? What does the devil use today to tempt humans? How possible is it for humans to withstand temptation without God's help?

● Watch television for an evening. Count how often people are tempted to do the wrong thing. Count how many times they withstand or give in to temptation. What lesson does the Bible teach concerning temptation?

● Pray the Lord's Prayer. Read Matthew 6:13 on its own, then read the entire prayer Jesus used to teach us to pray (Matthew 6:9-13). Why do you think temptation is mentioned in that common prayer?

## STAFF You'll Need

◯ Contact a video buff who doesn't mind being sly and sneaky.

## STUFF You'll Need

◯ video camera and tapes

◯ box or blanket for the "cover-up" to hide the video camera

◯ giant bowl of kid-pleasing candy

◯ crayons or markers

◯ children's coloring books or coloring pages

# MAKING IT HAPPEN

Teenagers will see how easy—or difficult—it is to resist temptation when they put together a tempting scenario something like this:

Arrange for a small group of children to meet around a table in a small room in which you've hidden a "spy eye"—a video camera disguised in a box or under a blanket. You'll need to use the teenagers' ingenuity to hide your camera so the small children don't suspect anything.

Provide crayons, markers, and coloring pages. But here's the kicker: Place a giant bowl of mouth-watering, kid-pleasing candy in the center of the table. Make sure your hidden camera is on before children enter the room.

Tell the children you would like for them to color the pages for you. Say that you need to leave for a while, but you'll check back. Say, **"Whatever you do, please don't eat the candy."**

Leave the children alone for six to ten minutes.

For fun, send in one of the other teenagers to see how the children are doing on their coloring assignment. Have the teenager dramatically grab a handful of candy, yum and ooh over it, open up any wrappers, and enjoy it in front of the children. (You're guaranteed to get a great reaction for the camera!)

If possible, rotate different groups of children into your spy-cam room.

Once you've collected enough footage, have fun gathering around the screen to see what unfolded. Edit the footage for interesting and funny comments to reveal kids' resistance to temptation. (Check with the children's parents to make sure they agree to let the footage of their kids be shown in church.) Remember to keep it short for impact and use in the pastor's sermon.

## Our Own "AH-HA's" :-)

When our pastor "set up" the temptation scenario of children in a closed room with a giant bowl of candy, the whole congregation cracked up. Just the thought of little kids and candy blared "temptation" big time! Of course, many people knew the children, so it was extra fun and funny.

To our surprise, the children obeyed and didn't give in to temptation. The children taught youth and adults that it is possible to resist temptation. With God's help, people *can* make good choices, resist temptations, and avoid painful consequences.

# CALLING ALL CARPENTERS

Hint: Combine this with Ah-Ha 18, "Artists' Corner" (p. 50), for a dynamic duo.

Build outdoor crosses and a frame to display artwork of Jesus' journey to the cross.

## BALLOT BLURB

☐ How about using wood and nails to build crosses for a dynamic outdoor display? Plus, construct a frame for the "Artists' Corner" masterpieces.

## SCRIPTURE LIFE CONNECTIONS

● Turn the entire building project into a Bible study using the idea contained on the following page. (Experience Mark 15:25-30 and Acts 2:23-24.)

● Prepare for Easter. This idea works especially well during Lent or the weekend before Easter.

## STAFF You'll Need

◯ Nail down any carpenters you know who love teenagers and want to see them grow in their understanding of Jesus' sacrifice.

## STUFF You'll Need

◯ lumber: 2x4s or 4x4s

◯ saws

◯ nails

◯ purple, black, and white cloth to hang on the center cross (optional)

# MAKING IT HAPPEN

Before striking the first nail, read Mark 15:25-30 as each teenager (gently!) presses a nail into the palm of his or her hand. Lead students in visualizing the pain, suffering, and mockery that Jesus endured as he hung on a cross between two robbers. Pray that God would use your carpentry skills to show people Christ's ultimate gift of love when he gave his life for us.

Plan how you'll show a perspective of three crosses outside your church. Determine the size and lumber needed. Figure out how you'll make them free-standing. Build away! We purposely leave the details up to you to fit your space needs.

Include plans for a free-standing frame that will be an art gallery. Use your creative genius to think of a way to link the crosses outside with the wooden frame that will transform your church's entrance into an art gallery. Plan ways to attach the artwork provided by the "Artists' Corner" (see Ah-Ha 18). Both these projects can be done separately, but they make for a great two-part project.

Never underestimate the nail as a powerful symbol. Take note of the faith witness in Acts 2:23-24 as disciples retold the story of Jesus' death and resurrection.

Next read John 20:24-28 in which Thomas demanded to see the nail marks in Jesus' hands. And when Thomas did touch Jesus' hands, he believed. Discuss how nails symbolize death, salvation, and belief.

Assign kids to be responsible for hanging the colored cloths on the cross, if you decide to do that. Decide if you want it up all week or just certain days. That decision may depend on the weather in your part of the country.

## Our Own "AH-HA's" :-)

Prior to Easter, the outdoor crosses became a bold, drive-by witness of Christ's sacrifice. Plus, it was a great way to involve men with youth in our congregation.

## weblink Get Graphics & Ballot Blurbs Online!

Designing your own ballots? Go to **www.grouppublishing.com/ creativefaithahhas/ballotextras** to download the illustrations used in this book as well as the ballot blurbs for all 45 Ah-Ha's.

# WORSHIP IN MOTION

### Choreograph a worship dance to the Lord.

## ScriptureLIFE connections

- Step into the Scriptures to see how God's people danced in praise. Prior to selecting a worship song, leap into Ecclesiastes 3:1, 4, where it says there's a time for everything—even a time to dance.

- Skip back to Exodus 15:19-21 for a glimpse of Miriam dancing in praise after the Israelites made it across the Red Sea on dry ground.

- Next walk through Psalm 30:11-12 and Psalm 149:1-4 for psalms that mention praising God with dance.

### BALLOT BLURB

☐ Offer a special treat that puts worship in motion. Design creative movement to music that will help people see God in a new way.

## STAFF You'll Need

◯ Find a choreographer, cheerleader, drama type, or creative musician who would like to design movement to music.

## STUFF You'll Need

◯ music selection

◯ CD and CD player

◯ clothing that matches, so you look like "many moving as one" (optional)

# MAKING IT HAPPEN

Teenagers train to use dance to express themselves in lots of settings. They participate in dance teams, flag teams, ballet classes. Why not channel that expertise and use it to God's glory?

Have dancers choose the song(s) they would like to use to glorify the Lord. Prior to song selection, read the Bible verses in the "ScriptureLife" section.

No matter how many students sign up for this Ah-Ha, it works! From a single ballet dancer to a large group in synchronized creative movement, this expression of worship can be powerful.

## MUSIC IDEAS
### for Creative Movement

If you want some ideas to jump-start your planning, here's a list of Christian songs that work well. (Thanks to our friend Cindy Hansen, who uses creative movement in worship with all ages. Our favorite is moms and daughters!)

- "Great Adventure" and "Lord of the Dance" by Steven Curtis Chapman on his *Greatest Hits* CD

- "Jump Into the Light," "Fixin' My Eyes on You," and "The People Shout, Hosannah!" by Jana Alayra on her *Jump Into the Light* CD

- "Hush" and "Softly and Tenderly" by Acappella on their *The Collection* CD

- "I'll Lead You Home" and "Crown Him With Many Crowns" by Michael W. Smith on his *I'll Lead You Home* CD

- Any songs from *Songs From the Loft*

## Our Own "AH-HA's" :-)

This idea seemed most foreign to our kids. Only two girls signed up. But their simple, self-designed choreography really added to our worship service. It was tastefully done and made an impact.

Each year during our summer workcamp programs, we incorporate small and large groups of students who use dance to express their faith.

## "UH-OH's"

### (Mistakes we made, so you don't have to.)

If this is new to your churchgoers, you may want to introduce creative movement with Scripture. Explain how God uses our bodies to demonstrate our thanks and praise.

# BUTTERFLY FACTORY

## 22

Create a mass of butterflies to give away as Easter gifts to families who come to worship Easter morning.

## BALLOT BLURB

☐ No one will forget Easter this year! You'll help plan and create bunches of beautiful butterflies to symbolize new life in Christ.

## SCRIPTURE LIFE CONNECTIONS

● Jesus said, "I am the resurrection and the life," to show us who he is. Look up John 11:25 and see for yourself.

● Open up to 2 Corinthians 5:17 for the perfect butterfly verse: "Therefore, if anyone is in Christ, he is a new creation; the old has gone, the new has come!" Wow! Use this verse to help teenagers see that Jesus' resurrection isn't just about Jesus; it's about us, too.

## STAFF You'll Need

◯ Bring together adults who love crafts.

## STUFF You'll Need

◯ one clothespin per family unit expected to attend Easter services (the wooden kind with a spring so it closes)

◯ a variety of colored tissue paper

◯ brightly colored chenille wires (one per clothespin) for antennae

◯ watercolor markers

◯ scissors

◯ glue gun and glue

# MAKING IT HAPPEN

Nothing symbolizes the miraculous new-life transformation of Easter better than a beautiful butterfly. Point that out to your "Butterfly Factory" workers, and ask them for reasons a butterfly makes a great symbol for Jesus' resurrection.

Read Jesus' words in John 11:25. Then make the human-"butterfly" connection by celebrating 2 Corinthians 5:17. Talk about what that means for each of them as Christians.

Depending on how many factory workers you have, consider setting up a mass production assembly line. Have kids take the following roles:

*Wing-makers*—Set out the colored tissue paper, scissors, and watercolor markers. Cut and design wings to fit the clothespin body.

*Wing-beautifiers*—Decorate the tissue wings with colorful squiggles and dots. Here's the job for doodlers.

*Body-builders*—Use a chenille wire to form a body that wraps around the tissue wings. Create antennae by crisscrossing and wrapping the wires at the top.

*Butterfly clippers*—Gather each butterfly body and hot glue it to the hinged clothespin so people can clip the butterflies on bulletin boards, plants, or other items for Easter reminders.

Collect and count the completed butterflies. Assign which teenagers will help hand out their celebratory symbols of the most important Christian holiday of all!

## Our Own "AH-HA's" :-)

We played upbeat Christian music while the factory workers buzzed away.

We liked this project because it could accommodate a large number of teenagers. This is great, especially if you have a larger church and expect a good number of families on Easter. It still seems true that more people attend as C and E Christians (Christmas and Easter), so give them a reminder to come back soon!

## "UH-OH's"
### (Mistakes we made, so you don't have to.)

Looking back, we may have missed an opportunity to clip to the butterfly a Bible verse or an invitation to upcoming church events to build on the excitement of Easter.

# 23 EASTER CROSS IN BLOOM

### Bring vibrant life to the cross with fresh flowers.

**BALLOT BLURB**

☐ Be part of a "transformation" project. Build a cross to hold fresh flower offerings on Easter morning.

## SCRIPTURE LIFE CONNECTIONS

● Bring Colossians 2:13-14 to life as worshippers watch the cross transform from death to life.

## STAFF You'll Need

◯ See if a florist or gardener-type would like to help with this.

## STUFF You'll Need

◯ large free-standing cross (If you've done Ah-Ha 20, "Calling All Carpenters" [p. 54], you could use the cross built for that.)

◯ chicken wire

◯ wood stapler and staples

◯ florist moss

◯ fresh flowers

◯ camera (optional)

# MAKING IT HAPPEN

Create a chicken wire "covering" for your cross by molding and stapling chicken wire to the entire cross. Then stuff florist moss into the wire everywhere.

Set up the cross in the front of the church for the first Easter worship service. You're right—it will look rough, unfinished, and downright ugly. That's where the transformation begins!

A few weeks prior to Easter, ask people to bring fresh flowers from home on Easter morning. Have teenagers greet people as they arrive and direct them to use their flowers to adorn the cross. Have extra flowers on hand for worshippers who arrive flowerless, so everyone can add to the cross.

Station helpers next to the cross to assist people of all ages as they bring their flower offerings. Tuck the stems into the wire and moss, and get ready for an awesome sight.

Watch the "dead" cross come to life as it's adorned with vibrant, colorful flowers.

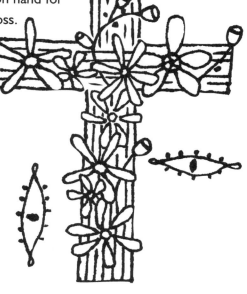

Be prepared for this to become an Easter tradition. The first year, people came up after the service to take pictures of the cross and family photos beside the cross. Now they bring their cameras for sure.

Oh! It smells good too! We have a great mother-daughter team that has now taken on this cross project as their contribution to the Easter service.

(Mistakes **we** made, so you don't have to.)

We could do a better job publicizing this experience. It's good to remind people again and again to bring flowers. Although we supply cut flowers for anyone, planning to bring a "new-life flower offering" makes a great discussion starter for churchgoing families, even before they get to the Easter service.

# AH-HA 24

# BODY-of-CHRIST BANNER BUNCH

### Create a banner to represent your church.

## BALLOT BLURB

☐ You'll create an awesome banner representing our church's families.

## SCRIPTURE LIFE CONNECTIONS

● Bring 1 Corinthians 12:12-27 to life with this banner project. Follow the devotional outline on the following page for deeper impact.

## STAFF You'll Need

◯ Be on the look out for someone who loves arts, crafts, or sewing. Or you may use this as a way to connect youth to a group in your church that designs banners year round.

## STUFF You'll Need

◯ large solid-colored felt or burlap background

◯ crosses collected from your church families (see the cross pattern on p. 116), or fabric scraps as a backup plan

◯ glue

◯ wooden dowel or other way to hang the banner for display

# MAKING IT HAPPEN

Design a banner to visually portray the diversity of the body of Christ representing your congregation.

For a month before your banner-making team begins, advertise the need for a cloth cross from each family in your church. Provide a pattern (see sample on page 116) and explanation of your banner project. You can adjust the size of your cross depending on the size of your congregation—meaning the larger the church, the smaller the crosses you need.

Once you've received the crosses, measure a felt or burlap background to accommodate all your crosses. Ask a seamstress, math expert, or engineer (!) for advice in calculating the exact size you'll need.

Begin your banner-making extravaganza with a Bible study. Use 1 Corinthians 12:12-27.

Set out the background material with the families' crosses all around the outside of it. Then read 1 Corinthians 12:12-13. Ask:

• **How is what's before us like or unlike the body of Christ?**

Get up and scatter the crosses all over the place. Pause and reflect on what has just happened to what you see. Now read 1 Corinthians 12:14-26. Ask:

• **How are our scattered crosses like or unlike our own church as the body of Christ?**

After discussing, have everyone bring the crosses back and place them on the background. (It's OK if they're clumped or disorganized at this point.) Ask:

• **How do you feel now about this symbol of our church?**

Join hands around your reassembled banner. Pray that God uses your banner as a strong portrayal of the body of Christ. Conclude by reading 1 Corinthians 12:27.

Jump into arranging the crosses on the banner. Then glue each cross into position. Attach the banner to a dowel for hanging.

If you plan to involve the entire congregation, allow plenty of time to get the word out. Advertise the cross pattern multiple times, multiple places, multiple ways. The more people hear about it, the more apt they are to participate. Get teenagers to announce their need for the crosses. Have them explain the project to build enthusiasm. Build in the time you need so you won't be frustrated because it's last minute.

The banner can become a keepsake for the whole church, just like a family heirloom quilt.

We've done this a couple of ways. At the church I (Joani) worked in before coming here, families created incredible representations of themselves and what symbolized their uniqueness as a family. Some used cloth from a special garment or quilt, photos of each family member, drawings, or attachments that represented hobbies or other special interests. It was really cool!

We've also done this and used fabric scraps from the church's quilting ladies. Teenagers traced handprints to represent each family unit in our church. This way the banner represented the entire church without needing to worry if families would participate.

Either approach works. And both show a "patchwork quilt" of diversity.

# THANKSGIVING MURAL MANIA

### Surround your worship area with a mural of thanks.

## BALLOT BLURB

☐ Display your artistic talents and give thanks to God at the same time. You'll design a gargantuan mural to surround your worship area.

## SCRIPTURELIFE CONNECTIONS

● Showcase the words of 1 Chronicles 16:8-10, and bring David's words of praise into a present-day context.

● Talk about what each phrase looks like today.

## STAFF You'll Need

○ Find the most thankful artist you can!

## STUFF You'll Need

○ giant roll of newsprint

○ tempera paints (Hint: When you add a smidgen of detergent to the paint, spills will clean up easier.)

○ assorted paintbrushes and sponge brushes

○ aluminum pie tins to hold the paint

○ newspapers as spill catchers

# MAKING IT HAPPEN

A giant roll of newsprint will supply the unlimited canvas for your Thanksgiving mural. Make sure you have enough to completely circle your worship area. That'll create the biggest impact and "wow." Place the newsprint on the floor so teenagers can gather around it to paint. You may want to add newspapers around the edges to absorb accidental splashes and splotches.

Before you begin painting, read 2 Corinthians 9:11-15. The words tell of our overflowing thanks for God's "indescribable gift." Let the mural be a way to express God's grace in pictures and words.

Brainstorm together all the things for which you're thankful. Begin with a prayer of thanks. Then paint away!

Because the mural is so vast, it forces artists to look deeper and deeper into things for which they're thankful. Encourage teenagers to add favorite Scripture passages that express God's grace and goodness.

Tape up the mural, and use it as a thank you prayer you can see.

## weblink Get Graphics & Ballot Blurbs Online!

Designing your own ballots? Go to **www.grouppublishing.com/ creativefaithahhas/ballotextras** to download the illustrations used in this book as well as the ballot blurbs for all 45 Ah-Ha's.

## Our Own "AH-HA's" :-)

It's fun to be surrounded by a visual thank you prayer during worship! And it's fun to watch people survey the teenagers' Thanksgiving masterpiece.

65

# RESPONSIVE PRAYERS

Write a prayer for the whole church
to pray together.

**BALLOT BLURB**

☐ Put your creative talents into high gear. Write a prayer for the entire congregation to pray together.

## SCRIPTURE LIFE CONNECTIONS

● Pray continually. When people gather to pray, there is power. Review the words in 1 Thessalonians 5:16-18. Let those verses guide the prayers and prayer-writers.

● Pray together. Ephesians 2:19-22 mentions that we are no longer foreigners but fellow citizens of God's household, his family. When the entire congregation prays together, it signifies the unity of spirit and oneness in Christ.

### STAFF You'll Need

◯ Look for someone who enjoys creative writing and who also believes in the power of prayer.

### STUFF You'll Need

◯ Bibles
◯ paper and pens
◯ method to put the finished prayer into print for the congregation. You might print paper copies, put it on an overhead transparency, or use PowerPoint to project it on a screen.

# MAKING IT HAPPEN

Begin with prayer. Ask God to guide your prayer-writing project. Provide Bibles, and choose a theme and direction for a responsive prayer. You may want to coordinate with your pastor for this.

Examples for themes might include:

- a prayer of thanks,
- praise and adoration,
- confession of sins, or
- prayers for others.

Examples of directions might include:

- Jesus, the Light of the World;
- world peace;
- unity of the body; or
- living water.

Another option is to use Scripture to guide you. Have students write responsive prayers inspired by the psalms. You might create a prayer based on one of the following psalms, using words and examples that teenagers would use today.

- Psalm 8 (Write a prayer of praise for God's majesty and our place in God's creation.)
- Psalm 51:1-12 (Write a prayer asking for forgiveness.)
- Psalm 103:1-22 (Write a prayer thanking God and giving God credit for all he does.)
- Psalm 100:1-5 (Write a prayer of joy and celebration.)

*Responsive* means that one leader or group will speak, then another. The prayer can be written to alternate speakers and groups of speakers. For example, a variation on Psalm 100 might look like this:

| | |
|---|---|
| All: | **Shout for joy to the Lord, everybody shout!** |
| Girls: | **We're glad, God!** |
| Guys: | **We're joyful, Lord!** |
| Leader: | **Know that the Lord is God.** |
| All: | **That's right.** |
| Girls: | **God, you made us!** |
| Guys: | **God, you made us!** |

You get the idea. Let God's Word inspire your prayers.

Once you've worked together to create a prayer, type it and make copies for the worshippers. Or prepare to present it in another way, such as PowerPoint or an overhead transparency.

# CHRISTMAS ANGELS

### Identify and adopt families who have special needs this Christmas.

**Hint:** Combine this with Ah-Ha 28 "Christmas Angel Video Documentary" (p. 70).

## BALLOT BLURB

☐ You can be an angel! Yes, you! You'll help identify families in need, fill in special handmade tree ornaments with each family's name and "need" description, and hang the ornaments on the tree for congregation members to adopt. You'll work closely with other "angel teams."

## SCRIPTURELIFE CONNECTIONS

● "Don't be afraid." That's what angels had to say when they appeared to humans. In this "Christmas Angels" project, your teenagers can tell families that they need not be so afraid this season. You can not only bring good news of God's love to them but also meet some of their physical needs.

● You may want to join the other teams from Ah-Ha's 28 ("Christmas Angel Video Documentary," p. 70) and 39 ("Food Baskets for the Needy," p. 94) for a joint "Angel" Bible study.

● Form teams and read the following famous angel accounts. Look for similarities and differences between the stories:
1. An angel appears to Mary in Luke 1:26-33.
2. An angel appears to Joseph in Matthew 1:18-21.
3. An angel appears to the shepherds in Luke 2:8-11.
4. An angel appears to the women at the tomb in Mark 16:1-7.

● Discuss how your teenagers can be "angels" to needy families this season.

## STAFF You'll Need

○ Find volunteers who have a heart for people in need and who want to mobilize teenagers into action.

○ Van drivers for one team per van. Parents make great recruits. Plus, it's a great way to involve parents in outreach with their teenagers.

## STUFF You'll Need

○ list of families in need and how to contact them

○ copies of the angel ornament pattern (p. 117)

○ markers, pens, ribbon

○ small Christmas tree

○ phones

# MAKING IT HAPPEN

You'll be part of the organizing force to make a difference in your community. Build a list of local families in need. Contact your pastor, church office, or local social services agency for names, addresses, and phone numbers (if possible) of needy families. Choose people who've experienced hardships financially (loss of jobs), emotionally (loss of loved ones to death or prison), and physically (loss of health or abilities). They may be lonely elderly folks or single-parents. Make sure they are willing to accept help from your church.

Form "angel teams." As a team-building activity, have students cut out, decorate, and fill in information about "adoptable" families on the angel ornaments. (See handout on page 117.)

Once you've listed all the families on the ornaments, have each team choose which family it wants to adopt. Then involve even more families in serving by inviting the congregation to join in too. Place the Christmas tree in a prominent spot, and hang the ornaments on it to alert the congregation to the opportunity to serve.

Ask for volunteers to call their adopted families and set up times to visit during the next couple weeks. You might propose a schedule like this:

*Week 1—Get acquainted.*

Find out the family's story, share who you are, and learn how you might help. Interview the family with questions and phrases like this:

- **Tell us your names and some of your favorite activities.**
- **Tell us your favorite foods.** (Keep note of that for special surprises later.)
- **Tell us about your family.**
- **What has been especially difficult for you lately?**
- **What would be helpful for us to do for you?**

*Week 2—Plan with your team.*

Recap what you learned last week. What ideas do you have for helping? Divide up responsibilities. For example, someone may want to go grocery shopping, someone else may want to buy socks and a sweatshirt for someone in the family, or someone else may volunteer to help clean the family's kitchen. Each plan will be unique to the needs of the family.

*Week 3—Return with gifts and goodies.*

Make sure your adopted family will be at home. Meet together and present your gifts. Be prepared. This could be an emotional time for all involved. Spend time talking and, if possible, volunteer to pray with the family.

If you're combining this with the "Christmas Angel Video Documentary" team (Ah-Ha 28), make sure the family gives you permission to videotape. We asked, and almost every family said it was OK.

Our Own "AH-HA's" :-)

This project turned into a tear-jerker. One woman was moved to tears when she saw the love and care from the teenagers. She couldn't believe that people who barely knew her would give so freely.

If possible, do combine this activity with Ah-Ha 28, the "Christmas Angel Video Documentary." That way the entire church can witness the power of this project.

# CHRISTMAS ANGEL VIDEO DOCUMENTARY

**Hint:** Combine this with Ah-Ha 27 "Christmas Angels" (p. 68).

Make a video documentary of the "Christmas Angel" project.

## BALLOT BLURB

☐ Become part of a video camera crew for filming "on location." You'll capture your peers reaching out to families in need with the heartwarming "Christmas Angel" project. You'll show the congregation God's love in action.

## SCRIPTURELIFE CONNECTIONS

- Join with the "Christmas Angel" team's Bible study about angels. See page 68.

- Sometimes the only way others can "travel" to new places is to view them on a screen. View your videotaping as a unique ministry.

- Read Ephesians 1:18 as a prayer for your video team: "I pray also that the eyes of your heart may be enlightened in order that you may know the hope to which he has called you, the riches of his glorious inheritance in the saints." Continue with Ephesians 1:19-23 for the full effect. As a video team, discuss how God can use you to "enlighten the eyes of hearts" to see hope in Jesus through this project.

## STAFF You'll Need

◯ Locate a leader who enjoys videotaping and editing. Think of this project as a news report "on location."

◯ Recruit drivers who can haul equipment and kids. You might round up a few dads to join in the fun!

## STUFF You'll Need

◯ video cameras, tapes, and editing equipment

# MAKING IT HAPPEN

As a video documentary crew, you'll work closely with the "Christmas Angels" team. They'll be organizing meeting with the families. (See page 68.)

Since this is a documentary, plan to capture the entire process from start to finish. You don't want to miss a thing. Videotape the planning, phoning, visiting to get acquainted with the families, and the gift giving. Also collect individual interviews from students and family members. You can intersperse the interviews when you edit the video.

Plan how your crew will operate. So that teams run smoothly, assign each person a job: Interviewer, Camera Operator, Grip (the one who helps carry stuff), and Logger (the one who'll keep notes of what's shot when and where). Hey, this makes editing a lot easier!

Depending on how many teams will be visiting families, plan to have multiple video crews. Chances are you'll need to provide your own transportation to sites.

Follow a few hints for editing your documentary. Be brutal—with the footage, not each other. Cut extraneous stuff. Find the most poignant and fun moments. Boil down the video to the most interesting and insightful segments. Make the video available to your entire congregation so they can see your ministry of caring.

## Our Own "AH-HA's" :-)

All the participants were touched by the power of this project. Kids reached out to real people in real need. One mom shared her life story of abuse and hardship (her husband is in prison). During the interview, she got all choked up, overwhelmed by the caring teenagers—"good kids" who wanted to help her.

That moment definitely made it on the final video. The documentary project helped bring youth ministry to the entire church.

# DESIGNER BULLETIN COVERS

## Supply the congregation with specially designed bulletin covers.

☐ Let your artistic talents shine. Design bulletin covers for the entire congregation to enjoy.

## SCRIPTURE LIFE CONNECTIONS

● Depending on the time of year and sermon series, this project can visually reflect any upcoming Scripture passages.

## STAFF You'll Need

○ Locate an artist or computer graphics specialist.

## STUFF You'll Need

○ paper

○ pencils, pens, markers

○ photocopier

○ computer with graphics program (optional)

# MAKING IT HAPPEN

Choose a specific number of weeks for which you'll design bulletin covers. Find out the worship themes, Scriptures, and whatever will help guide the process in visually representing those ideas. Check on the dimensions you have to work with. Decide if you'll design to those specifications or if you can later shrink or enlarge your masterpieces to fit the required format.

Be sure your designs will copy properly. Sometimes thin, wispy pencil drawings don't reproduce as well as bold lines. Decide if you'll use the church's copy machine or spring for a Kinko's job.

Communication is key. Find out how many copies you'll need, and coordinate with the church secretary or the person responsible for making the bulletins each week.

Be sure to give credit to the artists who design each week. And, if you can, have teenagers help distribute the bulletins on those weeks.

Homespun designs for bulletin covers helped create a "family feel" along with honoring young artists in our midst. Each week held a surprise visual that teenagers had designed.

# CHURCH IMPROVEMENT

### Do miscellaneous repair jobs around the church.

☐ You've heard of *Home Improvement*? Well, this is Church Improvement! Here's where you'll use your carpentry and painting skills to freshen up the church.

## SCRIPTURELIFE CONNECTIONS

● Check out the splendor and detail of Solomon's Temple. Read 1 Kings 6:1-38 for an outline of Solomon's seven-year building project in which he built God's house.

● Compare and contrast the detail described in the Bible with the workmanship of your church. Talk about how God looks at his house on earth.

● For a real twist, read 1 Corinthians 3:16-17; 6:19-20 and talk about how our bodies are the temple of the Holy Spirit. What does that understanding mean for "church improvement"?

## STAFF You'll Need

○ Nail down the person or committee that's responsible for the upkeep of your church property. Invite them to compile jobs that young people can do. Then ask if they would like to supervise a team of ambitious helpers. Encourage them to provide some tasks beyond painting and cleaning, based on the skills of your teens.

## STUFF You'll Need

○ building supplies such as hammers, nails, sandpaper, paint, paint scrapers, paintbrushes, dropcloths, whatever you need for your particular job

# MAKING IT HAPPEN

Partner with the people at your church who take care of the facility. Chances are a walk-through of the church together will highlight odd jobs teenagers could do. Consider paint touch-ups or complete rooms that need painting. Check out bathrooms, church nurseries, mailboxes, and hallways.

Pinpoint areas of need, collect supplies, and unleash your teenage church-improvement crew.

## Our Own "AH-HA's" :-)

Our kids removed wallpaper and repainted an outdoor mailbox. Even though the jobs were "behind the scenes," they helped improve our church in a special way.

## "UH-OH's"
(Mistakes **we** made, so you don't have to.)

Make sure you have enough work for students who sign up for the jobs, so that they'll feel valued. At times some of the tasks we did left kids standing around doing nothing. And that spells boredom.

**weblink** Get Graphics & Ballot Blurbs **Online!**

Designing your own ballots? Go to **www.grouppublishing.com/ creativefaithahhas/ballotextras** to download the illustrations used in this book as well as the ballot blurbs for all 45 Ah-Ha's.

# AH-HA 31

# CHRISTIAN CAREER PATHS

## Invite Christian ministry guests to tell about their calling.

☐ Meet real people who do real ministry. Find out if a full- or part-time ministry job is for you.

CAREER LADDER

## SCRIPTURELIFE CONNECTIONS

● Examine what the Bible says about ministry positions. See how 1 Corinthians 12:28-31 sheds light on this.

● Turn to Ephesians 4:11-13. Zero in on verse 12: "To prepare God's people for works of service, so that the body of Christ may be built up until we all reach unity in the faith and in the knowledge of the Son of God and become mature, attaining to the whole measure of the fullness of Christ." Discuss how God plans to use each of us, no matter what our vocation may be. Find out if being in ministry is God's plan for some of your students.

## STAFF You'll Need

◯ **Brainstorm your own list of ministry positions:** pastor, youth minister, children's minister, family minister, director of Christian/religious education, music minister, director of outreach, Christian teacher, missionary, nurse, and so on.

◯ **Choose which different positions you'd like to highlight.** Your choices might depend on the ministry professionals you know. (This is a great way to involve your senior pastor, too!) Invite a number of ministry representatives of your choice to talk with students.

## STUFF You'll Need

◯ I ballot per student, containing the ministry positions you're highlighting (See our sample on page 118.)

◯ I personalized schedule for each student, listing times and places for meeting their choices

◯ handouts of information on each ministry area (optional, prepared by presenters)

◯ whistle or bell to signal time to switch

# MAKING IT HAPPEN

Identify Christian career paths that require special training and know-how. Invite a spectrum of choices so kids see the variety that exists for ministry options. Then get out your Personal Digital Assistant, phone, e-mail, and address directory. Invite people to speak about their ministry calling. Ask each person (who represents a ministry area) to speak about his or her vocation and training for twenty to thirty minutes, depending on your schedule. Encourage the guests to tell about what they do, why they do it, and what kind of training is involved. Suggest that guests prepare handouts, videos, or whatever helps explain their passion for their calling.

Let people know that you'll set up a rotation plan, so students will travel from person to person according to the pre-arranged schedule. Prearranging a schedule helps you plan for room sizes and gives people who are presenting a heads-up as to how many handouts they might need.

Have your students choose as many careers to explore as you are able to allow them, taking your situation and timing into account. Collect kids' ballots, and divide the group into equal-size sessions that will rotate every twenty or thirty minutes.

Begin your "Christian Career Paths" fair by reading 1 Corinthians 12:4-6. Highlight the different gifts students are about to explore in the world of Christian careers.

Station each guest in a different room or a corner of a larger room. Hand students their Christian Career Path "travel plan" (otherwise known as their schedule), which tells them in which order to visit each guest. Use a whistle or bell to signal when it's time to rotate to a new station.

Have each guest provide a brief time for questions and answers at the end of his or her presentation. Remember, this is a time to expose kids to a variety of Christian careers. Because God has gifted everyone uniquely for his service, not all will be highly interested in the same choice. So exposure is the goal, not in-depth exploration. This experience can provide an opportunity to match students with interest areas later. Listen and watch for sparks of interest, and follow up!

(Mistakes **we** made, so you don't have to.)

It might have been interesting to record which careers kids were most interested in. We could have followed up and allowed students to dig deeper into their favorites.

## Our Own "AH-HA's" :-)

Not only was it fun to see what ministry careers intrigued students, but the whole event also affirmed the ministry professionals. It helps rekindle passion for ministry when you get to communicate to young people what God is doing through you and your vocation.

# 32 STUFF JOHN!

Design and show off a modern-day
John the Baptist.

## BALLOT BLURB

☐ John the Baptist got people's attention. So will you! Figure out how to make a life-size stuffed person to represent John, dress him up, and make cool signs for him to hold.

## SCRIPTURELIFE CONNECTIONS

● Investigate the message of John the Baptist and what made him such a peculiar prophet. Grapple with Jesus' return. Read what Jesus told the disciples about the end of the age in Luke 21:5-36.

● Focus on Jesus' advice in verse 36. What does it mean to "be always on the watch"?

## STAFF You'll Need

◯ Roust up an adult who has a good sense of humor and a few construction skills. Maybe you'll even want to involve a plumber who has access to some PVC pipe.

## STUFF You'll Need

◯ 1½-inch PVC pipe, lengths and joints

◯ Styrofoam "head"

◯ costuming to fit the themes you choose (clothes, wigs, hats)

◯ poster board, markers, and paint for signs (weather-proofing optional)

◯ hammer and stakes to stabilize the structure

# MAKING IT HAPPEN

John the Baptist got people's attention. And he dressed in scratchy camel hair and ate crunchy locusts. Yum. So why not capture some of John's attention-grabbing techniques and create a John the Baptist of your own? Think "scarecrow" in front of your church for three weeks before Christmas. You'll have teenagers build a free-standing wooden scarecrow frame to be your modern-day prophet, complete with odd clothing and large billboard signs. To build John, design a PVC-pipe skeleton. Use 1½-inch PVC pipe as bones, elbows, and connections.

To come up with your ideas for signs and wardrobe, begin with a Bible study on John the Baptist. Form four groups, assigning each group one of the Gospel passages that talk about him: Matthew 3:1-12; Mark 1:1-8; Luke 3:1-18; John 1:6-7, 15-26. Ask each group to create two lists from its passage: one list that describes John and a second list that describes John's message. Then compare the lists among groups, and decide what three main messages John proclaimed. If possible, tie your three messages into the pastor's sermon. We did, and it worked great!

Then let the Bible lists inspire ways to dress "John" and what words to use on the signs he'll hold. Have kids brainstorm three different get-ups for dressing John that match the message he'll proclaim each week. Form kids into three groups, one for decorating John each week; or two groups, one for wardrobe each week, the other for signage.

Here are the signs our teenagers made:

**Week 1 sign: PREPARE**

Get ready for action. John was prepared for attack in a karate outfit. Eee-yah!

**Week 2 sign: WATCH**

Ask any scarecrow in a cornfield watching for the birds. John's bib overalls, straw hat, and dreadlocks wig said, "Watch!"

**Week 3 sign: REJOICE**

John appeared quite happy decked out in a bright purple jacket. A jester's hat and sunglasses topped off his joyous ensemble.

In the three weeks leading up to Christmas, change John's wardrobe and sign each week to build intrigue and anticipation for Jesus' entry into the world.

## Our Own "AH-HA's" :-)

For many years we in the church have been notorious for taking ourselves too seriously. This project can't help but make people smile. Plus, it was a zany project for the kids to work on. And they'll never forget John the Baptist!

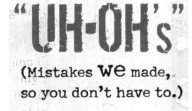

## "UH-OH's"

(Mistakes we made, so you don't have to.)

Each week's sermon tied into John's signs perfectly. But we could have done a better job calling attention to him and building curiosity for the next week's sermon. Corresponding artwork and signs inside the worship area would've helped too.

# AH-HA 33 GIANT TREASURE CHEST

### Design a treasure chest for worship offerings.

**BALLOT BLURB**

☐ Help build and decorate a giant, life-size treasure chest to hold our church's offerings.

## SCRIPTURELIFE CONNECTIONS

- Discuss what it means to have treasures in heaven. Unearth the message of Jesus in Matthew 6:19-21.

- Discuss what treasures we store up today and where students' time and money goes. How do our actions reflect or not reflect the words "For where your treasure is, there your heart will be also"?

- Let the challenge in Malachi 3:10 preface your treasure-chest building.

- This project sparks all kinds of themes concerning gifts, stewardship, and "buried treasure." Use what works best for you.

## STAFF You'll Need

- ◯ Recruit someone who deals with stewardship or finances.

- ◯ Add an artistic type to the leadership team.

## STUFF You'll Need

- ◯ giant treasure chest, trunk, or box

- ◯ whatever you need to decorate your treasure chest to make it look like it's dripping in jewels

- ◯ Bible study supplies including Bibles, resealable plastic bags, and an assortment of favorite candy

# MAKING IT HAPPEN

God lavishes gifts galore on us! What better symbol to show God's treasures than a treasure chest? If your church emphasizes stewardship, giving tithes and offerings, and making time and talent commitments, have teenagers create a visual reminder of God's bounty by building or decorating a giant treasure chest.

In preparation for designing the treasure chest, do a Bible study on giving. Prepare small resealable plastic bags filled with various kinds and amounts of kids' favorite candies. For example, fill one bag with Skittles, M&M's, a Snickers candy bar, Sweetarts, and licorice. Vary the candy type from bag to bag, and also vary the amount in each bag. Have some with assorted candies and others with all one kind. Imagine you're God doling out different gifts, talents, and finances. Give each student one of the bags. Listen for oohs and ahs and groans and whines. Bag-receivers will no doubt respond to the amount and kind of candy they receive.

Have everyone open his or her Bible and read Malachi 3:10. To illustrate what tithing (giving 10 percent) means, tell everyone to give back to you 10 percent of what you gave them. Watch and listen for "teachable moments." (And there'll be a lot!) Once everyone has "tithed," discuss:

- **How did you feel when I gave you your bag?**
- **How is that like how people feel about God's gifts to them?**
- **How is this experience like tithing your time, money, and talents back to God?**

Challenge students to make a commitment to tithe what they receive back to the Lord. For example, how many waking hours do they have in a week? How much money do they receive? What does giving back to God mean for them?

Brainstorm how to build and decorate the treasure chest. See if someone has an old trunk that would work, or talk about ways to use painted cardboard to design a treasure chest just the way you want it. Bring costume jewelry, and decorate the chest to create a wow-effect of beautiful buried treasure just discovered.

While you construct the treasure chest to hold your congregation's tithes and offerings, reflect on what a challenge it is to trust God with our tithes.

Involve the entire congregation in celebrating the gifts God has given them. Use the treasure chest to enhance worship in these ways:

- Place tithes and offerings inside.
- Drop in written notes that describe personal commitments to God.
- Write and deposit Thanksgiving notes for God's gifts.

## Our Own "AH-HA's" :-)

The treasure chest became a strong visual reminder of the treasures God gives us. People placed offerings and commitments inside.

The candy-bag Bible study evoked all kinds of discoveries. Some kids delighted in giving their candy away. Others felt cheated because they didn't get what they wanted or didn't get as much as they wanted. Besides being a fun way to make our point, the kids learned a bunch about tithing.

# GLITTER AND GOLD GIFT BAGS

**34**

Decorate and fill Christmas gift bags for children.

## SCRIPTURELIFE CONNECTIONS

- Read Luke 2:1-20 for the story of God's Son, Jesus—the ultimate gift of love.

- Unwrap the gifts of the Magi; hunt for insights in Matthew 2:1-11 and for the reason we would give gift bags in the first place.

## STAFF You'll Need

○ This idea calls for a few "bag ladies"—moms with an artistic streak and an ability to help teenagers fill bags with goodies.

## STUFF You'll Need

○ paper sandwich bags

○ Christmas goodies children will enjoy—peanuts, wrapped candies (hard or chocolate), apples, and oranges. (Get the entire congregation in the Christmas spirit, and ask for donations!)

○ selection of Bible verse gift tags and tape or ribbon for attaching

○ Christmas stickers, recyclable Christmas cards, glue, glitter, and markers to decorate bags

○ tempera paints and sponges in Christmas shapes (optional)

# MAKING IT HAPPEN

Involve youth in the joy of gift-making and gift-giving. Provide piles of Christmas stickers, old Christmas cards to cut up, glue, glitter, gold pens, markers—anything to add a festive touch to plain old paper sandwich bags. Have teenagers decorate the bags, one bag for every child anticipated to attend Christmas Eve or Christmas Day worship services.

Involve congregation members in the fun by requesting Christmas treats: peanuts in the shell, fresh oranges or apples, wrapped Christmas candy—anything that would delight little ones.

Once the bags are "Christmas-ized," create an assembly line to fill bags with the treats you've collected. You may want to designate some bags for children with allergies or other special health concerns. For example, label some bags "no peanuts" or "no chocolate."

Have bag decorators select favorite Bible verses and use them on gift tags for the bags. Christmas verses might include Luke 2:10; Luke 2:11; and Luke 2:14. To mass-produce the Scripture gift tags, create a sheet of Bible verses, printed and decorated; photocopy the sheet, cut the tags apart; and attach them to the bags with tape or ribbon.

Plan for teenagers' help to distribute the gift bags at your Christmas worship celebrations.

## "UH-OH's"
(Mistakes WE made, so you don't have to.)

Double-check with the children's ministry leaders to make sure they don't have any rules about certain foods for children. Some churches have banned peanuts because of children's allergies. By the way, parents can enjoy the contents as well as their children. A hidden benefit, don't you think?

## Our Own "AH-HA's" :-)

On a personal note, both of us remember (very fondly) the Christmas Eve treat bags we received from our churches when we were little children. Even though we grew up in different areas of the country, our childhood churches made that a fond memory for us. Those Christmas bags left an impression on us as children that our church was positive, exciting, and child-friendly. That's why we wanted to renew the children's goodie bag tradition in our church today!

# TELE-THANKERS

Call people on the telephone to find out
what they're thankful for.

## BALLOT BLURB

☐ Like to talk on the phone? Call church members and ask them what they're thankful for this year. We'll incorporate their thanks in the worship service.

## SCRIPTURELIFE CONNECTIONS

● Indescribable! 2 Corinthians 9:15 says, "Thanks be to God for his indescribable gift!" Have teenagers look extra close for indescribable gifts from God.

● View this as a roundabout ministry. See each phone conversation as a way to demonstrate the positive interaction described in Ephesians 5:19-21. Here's a way to speak to one another: always giving thanks.

## STAFF You'll Need

○ Round up someone who can organize and help record information.

## STUFF You'll Need

○ church phone directory list to divide among callers

○ telephones (cell phones will qualify too)

○ paper and pens to record answers

# MAKING IT HAPPEN

Arrange for a fleet of phones that kids can use. Cell phones count! Teenagers can really help rounding up enough phones. Have a church telephone directory handy, and divide up the names and numbers among the teenagers. Tell kids they'll be "tele-thankers," hunting for everything people are thankful for.

Write out a script so that students sound legitimate and professional. Say something like, **"Hi! I'm _____ calling from _____. We're collecting thank you thoughts from our church members to use as prayers in our worship service. We would like to know what you're most thankful for this year."** Remember to thank each person for talking with you. (It would be weird to make a phone call about thankfulness without thanking the caller!)

Make sure every caller jots down the answers received, and compile all of the answers.

Have another team of students input the thankful comments into a computer for use in worship. Decide if you want to attribute names to the list or leave the prayers anonymous. Connecting names with thanks helps build a family feel in your church. You could set up a computer to scroll the names and prayers on a screen, or you might just type up the list and distribute it as a handout.

Use the list of responses for a prayer during an upcoming worship service. Thanksgiving services are an obvious choice, but any time will work.

## "UH-OH's"
### (Mistakes WE made, so you don't have to.)

Looking back, we could have paved the way for this project by letting church members know they might be getting a call to find out what they're thankful for. Plus, we could've better advertised the upcoming presentation of the prayer collection.

## Our Own "AH-HA's" :-)

We found this to be a great, nonthreatening way to involve more people in prayer and giving thanks.

**weblink** Get Graphics & Ballot Blurbs Online!

Designing your own ballots? Go to **www.grouppublishing.com/ creativefaithahhas/ballotextras** to download the illustrations used in this book as well as the ballot blurbs for all 45 Ah-Ha's.

# PRAYER PATH PREP

**Hint:** Consider using this with Ah-Ha 37, "Prayer Path Promotions" (p. 90).

Prepare and host *The Prayer Path: A Christ-Centered Labyrinth Experience.*

## BALLOT BLURB

☐ Help create an awesome multimedia prayer experience. You'll collect props, design a unique labyrinth of experiential prayer stations, and host members of our community and church as they experience prayer in fresh and inviting ways.

## SCRIPTURE LIFE CONNECTIONS

● "Hear, O Lord," cried the psalmist David. Psalm 86, among many others, depicts the close communication between David and his God. Explore this psalm and others of your choosing to find biblical examples of prayer.

● Thematically, you can use this project as an all-out Prayer Extravaganza for your church. Thousands have experienced the way God works through *The Prayer Path.*

## STAFF You'll Need

○ Find a few adult leaders who will go the extra mile for this project. They'll need to lead teenagers in designing the labyrinth and in planning and coordinating the event.

## STUFF You'll Need

○ Purchase *The Prayer Path: A Christ-Centered Labyrinth Experience* from Group Publishing, Inc. (1-800-447-1070 or www.grouppublishing.com). For a closer look, go to www.grouppublishing.com/prayerpath to see snippets in action and read stories from those who've used it.

○ Read the leader guide in *The Prayer Path* resource for a detailed listing of supplies.

# MAKING IT HAPPEN

The power of this experience in youth ministry is worth the extra time and effort.

You'll need to purchase *The Prayer Path: A Christ-Centered Labyrinth Experience*. It's a big can filled with tools for making this experience happen. It contains complete instructions for designing a labyrinth with multimedia prayer stations and for facilitating its use.

The concept involves creating a "prayer walk" through the labyrinth during which participants experience eleven stations. For the journey, each person receives a personal Walkman CD player (imagine a self-guided museum tour), a *Prayer Path* CD, and a booklet. Once the CD begins, individuals go through *The Prayer Path* at their own pace, experiencing prayer at each station. For example, one station involves unloading your sin by tossing a stone into water; another involves lighting a candle and praying for a loved one. Again, the leader guide gives a clear outline of supplies needed and how to set up the experience.

More! →

*The Prayer Path* is self-guided and can last up to an hour if a person chooses. Each person can set his or her own pace, and multiple people can go through the experience at the same time, limited only by the number of CD players and CDs available.

When we did this, we got permission to use our church's fellowship hall for the six weeks preceding Easter so that we could semi-permanently tape the labyrinth walkways to the floor. This made setup and takedown during the week so much easier! (Thank you, church custodians!) The teenagers used black plastic tape to mark out the shape of the labyrinth design, which is clearly explained and illustrated in the leader guide.

In addition to building the labyrinth "walkway," have the students divvy up responsibility for supplies, which range from personal Walkman CD players to sand and rocks. Depending on how and when you plan to use *The Prayer Path,* assign students to be "hosts" who'll answer questions and help get participants started.

Our youth hosted *The Prayer Path* for the entire church and community. (See Ah-Ha 37 for "Prayer Path Promotions" [p. 90].) We had teams responsible for setup, takedown, and hosting each week.

## Our Own "AH-HA's" :-)

This takes work and planning, but the payoff is tremendous. All ages of youth and adults experienced it. We recall one very active middle school guy. We'll call him "Todd" here to protect his identity. Todd donned the Walkman headphones and began. We held our breath. Although the experience is active, the "activity" is quiet, reflective, and meditative. It was hard to imagine our exuberant friend would "get it." Were we wrong! Todd experienced the entire *Prayer Path* and was the most "reflectively prayerful" we'd ever seen him. When he had finished, he came up and asked, "Can I do that again?"

Todd wasn't the only one. God used this experience in powerful ways. We know that because each person makes an entry into a "guest book" at the conclusion. In it they write their impressions and how God touched them through *The Prayer Path* experience.

## "UH-OH's" :-O

(Mistakes we made, so you don't have to.)

The students went to a lot of work! We should have done so much more publicity to the community—and in our own church. So don't repeat the same mistake we did. Make sure you emphasize the value of the "Prayer Path Promotions," Ah-Ha 37 (p. 90). The posters we did create weren't strategically and broadly distributed. Because *The Prayer Path* consistently proves to be a powerful outreach to churched and unchurched alike, it's worth promoting—big time!

## And There's More! BONUS!

If the topic of prayer doesn't interest you or your group at this time, don't let that stop you from doing a project like this. Check out two similar power-packed multimedia events:

*Discovering Jesus*— Through a dynamic, multimedia tour through Jesus' birth, death, and resurrection, participants will be inspired to draw closer to Jesus and will experience God's presence in a powerful, potentially life-changing way.

*Walking in His Footsteps*—Journey with Jesus day-by-day through the last week of his life! This twelve station experience leads participants through events like Palm Sunday, Jesus' arrest and crucifixion, Resurrection Sunday, and two important post-Resurrection experiences. This compelling worship experience brings the Passion week to life.

Both are available at www.grouppublishing.com.

# PRAYER PATH PROMOTIONS

Design and deliver posters that advertise *The Prayer Path: A Christ-Centered Labyrinth Experience.*

**Hint:** Consider using with Ah-Ha 36, "Prayer Path Prep" (p. 86).

## BALLOT BLURB

☐ Use your design and marketing skills to plaster the community—and our church—with posters to tell the world about the power of prayer.

## SCRIPTURELIFE CONNECTIONS

● We talk a lot about sharing "the good news" with others. It's like we're all Christ-marketers. Look at getting the word out about God's generous love (from the perspective of advertising, marketing, and publicity). One way to reach out is to advertise what God does. As a "promotions" team, view your job as extremely important in letting others know about God's love and the power of prayer.

For fun, take a look at some early "advertisers" and "marketers." See the shepherds in Luke 2:15-20; John the Baptist in Luke 3:15-18 (verses 19-20 tell how marketing could get you in trouble!); Mary Magdalene in John 20:11-18; Peter in Acts 2:14-41. That names just a few.

● For even more fun, find other biblical examples of marketing the good news.

## STAFF You'll Need

◯ Advertise for someone with a spark for publicity, marketing, advertising, or sales.

## STUFF You'll Need

◯ posters and poster paraphernalia to make a big splash

◯ markers, poster paint, paintbrushes

# MAKING IT HAPPEN

This Ah-Ha will be a team effort. Work with the "Prayer Path Prep" team (Ah-Ha 36, p. 86). Your job entails designing a publicity plan and posters to get the word out about *The Prayer Path: A Christ-Centered Labyrinth Experience*. Oh, by all means, don't feel you need to limit your publicity plan to posters only. Brainstorm. And think big!

Gather your team. Give a pep talk, and do a Bible study. Fire up the team with the importance of its purpose. Pray together for guidance. Then make a plan.

Gather the information you need to create the posters and other advertising:

*The Prayer Path: A Christ-Centered Labyrinth Experience*
- **What:** An incredible journey with God; a prayer experience like none other. (Add "benefit" statements that you'll find included with the *Prayer Path* kit.)
- **When:**
- **Where:**
- **Who can come:**
- **Who is sponsoring it from your church:**

Figure out where you'll place the posters, and tally how many posters you'll need. Then let your creative poster-designers go wild. Once your posters are complete, decide how you'll "post" the posters and who'll be involved. Turn "posting" into a time for fun and friendship building. Maybe go out for pizza or burgers to celebrate getting the word out about the power of prayer. Thank God for your food, and pray that God would bless your efforts beyond your wildest imaginations.

Plan a time for your team to experience *The Prayer Path*. It will make all your hard work worth it.

## Our Own "AH-HA's" :-)

The poster-makers did a fantastic job displaying their creativity. My favorite: The poster with black and white splotches like cowhide that read, "Got Prayer?"

## "UH-OH's"
(Mistakes we made, so you don't have to.)

We wished we had been more strategic and thoughtful about publicity for the *Prayer Path* experience. Since we've told you our goof, don't do the same. Get the word out.

# SPIRITED MOBILE

Create a hanging mobile that resembles tongues of fire.

BALLOT BLURB

☐ Here's a spark of an idea that needs you. Make a mobile to celebrate the birthday of the church!

## ScriptureLIFE connections

● Hold a birthday party! Get fired up about the church's birthday by reading Acts 2:1-12. Imagine the scene: wind, fire, people talking funny—a wild party for sure!

● Next review Peter's bold address in the midst of being ridiculed: Acts 2:13-41.

● See how the church continued in Acts 2:42-47. And take note: The church hasn't stopped!

## STAFF You'll Need

◯ Check for any artists or art teachers who would like to join this project.

## STUFF You'll Need

◯ wood crosspiece for the top of the mobile

◯ craft foam (red, orange, and yellow make great fire colors)

◯ colored construction paper (optional, if the foam doesn't work for you)

◯ fishing line

◯ scissors and tape

◯ large needles that work with craft foam

◯ candle and matches

◯ Bible

◯ birthday cake and candles (optional)

To "set the stage" for this art project, gather in a dark place. Light one candle so you can see to read Acts 2:1-4. Talk about what it must have been like to be there when the Holy Spirit appeared in the way the passage describes. Give thanks to God for the Holy Spirit and the power he has.

In that spirit, brainstorm how to create a giant mobile to show floating tongues of fire that shimmer in the wind. Create a crosspiece that can hold fishing line and craft-foam flames. Depending on the size, experiment with how many flames you can support and how many varied lengths. Be as simple or as elaborate as you like. Cut out red foam flames. If you want to get fancy, add yellow and orange to the center of the red flame (both sides) or create an assortment of flame colors. You choose.

Thread a large needle to connect fishing line to each flame, and leave varying lengths of fishing line to connect the flame to the crosspiece hanger. It will take some creativity and experimenting to get the mobile to balance and to hang properly. If you hang it in an area with gentle air currents, the flaming mobile will flicker like flames.

Decide where to hang your masterpiece so that it might have the most impact. Somewhere front and center in the worship area might be most powerful.

One more idea: Bring a birthday cake with candles to celebrate your work on the mobile and the birthday of the church.

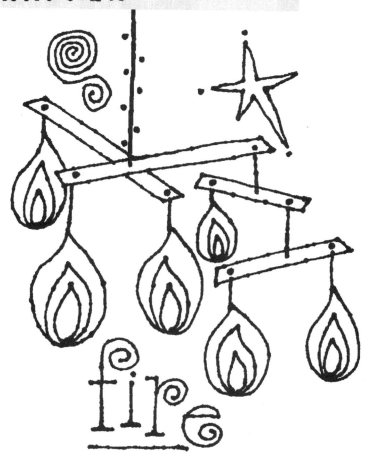

We created a giant mobile that hung from high, high up in the ceiling of our worship area. It hung down just above our heads as we walked down the center aisle. Gentle yet commanding—just like the Holy Spirit's presence.

# FOOD BASKETS FOR THE NEEDY

**Hint:** Couple this Ah-Ha with "Christmas Angels," Ah-Ha 27 (p. 68), for a cool Christmas project any time of the year.

### Collect and fill food baskets to give to needy families.

## BALLOT BLURB

☐ Help feed hungry families by collecting food, assembling food basket gifts, and delivering them.

## SCRIPTURELIFE CONNECTIONS

● Put Matthew 25 into action! Use Matthew 25:34-40 as food for thought. Have each person picture one specific person he or she believes is in need of food. When students have those people in mind, have them imagine Jesus disguised as each person who'll receive a food basket. How does that picture change your perspective of the food basket recipient? How does that change your perspective of Jesus?

● Examine the relationship between our faith and our actions. Discuss James 2:14-18. What does it mean to have faith without deeds? What does it mean to have deeds without faith?

## STUFF You'll Need

○ heavy-duty boxes or baskets
○ list of people in need and their addresses
○ notecards and pens
○ copies of the "We Need Food" handout (p. 119)
○ *Optional:* If you want to collect other items, expand your list to include:
● *toiletries:* shampoo, toothpaste, deodorant, toilet paper, tissue, razors, toothbrushes;
● *food items for the homeless:* canned meats (Spam, tuna, and so on), juice, fruit, pudding cups, crackers, granola bars, small boxes of cereal;
● *baby items:* formula, food, disposable diapers (large and extra large), baby wipes.

## STAFF You'll Need

○ Find a batch of caring adults who'll help organize the project.
○ Enlist drivers willing to deliver teenagers, food baskets, and a listening ear.

# MAKING IT HAPPEN

The basic idea involves collecting food, divvying it up, and delivering it. When you have your food collectors together, decide how you plan to creatively collect the food items. Spark your thinking with these ideas:

● Advertise your needs in the church newsletter or bulletin, or make posters to display.

● Do a canned food scavenger hunt by going door-to-door in neighborhoods.

● Ask each teenager to bring certain grocery items to build food baskets.

Once you've gathered all your food items, plan a food basket assembly-line party. Turn your gift-giving into a joyous occasion. Tie in the Bible study suggestions listed in the "ScriptureLife Connections." Use addresses and information to match baskets with families' needs. Include a signed notecard from your group. You may want to add Scripture, a prayer, and church information.

Place all the baskets and their cards in an area where your group can surround them to pray. Select baskets one by one and pray specifically for the family that will be receiving each food basket. Then load your food baskets and energetic teenagers into vehicles and head out. Don't forget a map!

When you arrive at each location, pause to pray and then deliver the basket.

If possible, spend time meeting the family members. If you're visiting a shut-in, your presence and listening ear may be as much of a gift as the food basket!

Our Own "AH-HA's" :-)

It's always overwhelming to see the outpouring of our church's generosity when we ask for food. We set up a table in the worship entrance for collecting items. The outpouring of gifts demonstrates a great lesson for our teenagers. They see tangible evidence of Christian love when others participate in these kind of projects.

# MUSIC VIDEO MAKERS

Make a music video to share with the congregation.

☐ Ever wanted to produce a music video? Here's your chance! You'll select a song with a Christian message and then produce a music video for all to see and hear!

## SCRIPTURELIFE CONNECTIONS

● Look at Psalm 40:3. Talk about how you'll be using "a new song." Especially note how this is an opportunity in which you hope "many will see and fear and put their trust in the Lord" (Psalm 40:3b).

● Discuss how you can use this video to show Jesus to people. Design a Bible study around the song you choose.

● Challenge teenagers to find Scriptures that support the song, and brainstorm how you're going to depict the song with visuals.

## STAFF You'll Need

◯ Enlist a video buff who knows camera work and editing, plus someone with a flair for visual choreography, staging, and drama.

## STUFF You'll Need

◯ video equipment: cameras, tapes, editing equipment

◯ various Christian CDs. *At the Foot of the Cross, Vol. I* is one we used. Another group used Ray Boltz's "Watch the Lamb."

◯ CD player

# MAKING IT HAPPEN

Bring on the music. Start with a listening session to choose one song to portray visually. Ask kids to jot down possible visual images as they listen to the songs.

Next "storyboard" how you want the song to look. Draw small pictures that depict various scenes. Plan locations, costumes, and setup. Let teenagers unleash their creativity to shoot and edit as they create their own blockbuster music video.

**To make sure you're within the legal boundaries when you create the video, we recommend that you directly contact the copyright holders for the song you select and request their permission to use the song as part of a public video presentation.**

## Our Own "AH-HA's" :-)

One of the videos we made was for use during worship before Easter. The video using Ray Boltz's "Watch the Lamb" played during the offering for Maundy Thursday. This Holy Week worship service celebrated communion and the night Jesus and his disciples ate the Passover meal—a perfect connection to Jesus, our ultimate Passover Lamb. This particular song helped students powerfully grasp the meaning between Jesus and the Old Testament Passover lamb.

The students chose a mix of present-day children (who happened to be our pastor's kids, so everyone recognized them) and our own worship area, combined with pictures of Jesus and scenes leading up to the crucifixion. Students added a shadowy hand using a hammer to pound nails, a local dirt road to show the road to Calvary, and other images. Because the song "Watch the Lamb" tells a story, it was fairly literal and worked well with junior highers.

**"UH-OH's" :-O**
(Mistakes we made, so you don't have to.)

We found it difficult for young teenagers to think abstractly, so that made it challenging at times. It's a reminder to use more concrete music for kids who think more concretely. Older teenagers can think a bit more creatively.

Another discovery? The longer the song, the more work it is to edit the video. You may want to keep that in mind too.

Be sure to plan ahead so all the students involved get in on the editing process. Schedule conflicts made it tough to reconvene everyone to complete the project. Therefore, the final stages fell to a dedicated few.

**weblink** Get Graphics & Ballot Blurbs **Online!**
Designing your own ballots? Go to **www.grouppublishing.com/ creativefaithahhas/ballotextras** to download the illustrations used in this book as well as the ballot blurbs for all 45 Ah-Ha's.

# RAISING THE ROOF BY LOWERING A FRIEND

## Lower a stretcher from the ceiling to illustrate a Bible story.

☐ Use your engineering skills to design a stretcher that will lower from the ceiling. Then you'll be able to make a Bible story unforgettable!

## SCRIPTURELIFE CONNECTIONS

● Make Mark 2:1-12 unforgettable. Read the Scripture passage, and discuss how far you would go to bring your friend to Jesus.

● Analyze what the group of friends must have been like to go to the lengths they did to lower their friend through the roof to see Jesus. Imagine what that experience must have been like.

● Take a deeper look at how Jesus "lowered" himself to save us from our sins. Have students look up Isaiah 53; Romans 5:6-8; and Philippians 2:5-11—passages that demonstrate God's willingness to sacrifice himself for us.

## STAFF You'll Need

○ This time you'll need an engineer-type who can assess your unique setting and design accordingly.

## STUFF You'll Need

○ wood, nails, fabric, and saws to create a stretcher

○ pulley system with ropes

○ bread, plate, and cup or chalice covered by white cloth (optional)

# MAKING IT HAPPEN

Study the Bible story in Mark. Have students discuss what it must have been like for people to defy all odds and get their friend to Jesus—through the roof. Spend some time imagining what that day must have been like. Pretend that suddenly you're all the friends of the paralyzed man and you need to lower someone through the roof. How would you accomplish that?

Brainstorm how you'll build a stretcher and a system that could lower what appears to be a person into your worship area. Maybe it's from a balcony area. Maybe it's from up front. You'll need to muster all your creativity and ingenuity to figure this one out. Work together to plan and build a stretcher that can be lowered during the story of the paralyzed man whose friends lowered him through the roof.

Coordinate with your pastor to use this as an unforgettable way to demonstrate the Mark 2 story. Assign kids who'll be the ones to actually run the system for the worship service. During the Scripture reading or storytelling, dramatically lower the stretcher from above. Guaranteed, you'll have jaws drop too!

If your church celebrates communion, tie the stretcher scene into a communion surprise. Have the bread and wine hidden on the stretcher under a white cloth, so people imagine a body as it lowers. What a great way to emphasize Christ lowering himself to offer his body and blood for us (1 Corinthians 11:23-26).

## Our Own "AH-HA's" :-)

When our church did this, the children performed a musical that told the story of the paralyzed man being lowered through the roof. During their song, ever so slowly, a stretcher high above at the front of the church slowly made its way down. Every eye was riveted on the stretcher. The creak, creak, creak sound of the rope through the pulley echoed as the stretcher inched its way to the floor.

Later, in the sermon, our pastor related how Jesus emphasized the power of forgiveness before he healed the paralytic. Then he walked over, lifted the cloth, and revealed the plate of bread and cup for Communion. Needless to say, it was a memorable way to introduce Jesus coming to us in a tangible way from above. Very powerful!

## "UH-OH's" :-O
### (Mistakes we made, so you don't have to.)

This really wasn't a mistake, but it was another way we thought about this. Our church does have a balcony and we had originally thought the stretcher might be lowered from there. That would've worked too. Sometimes it's interesting to have people turning around and craning their necks to see what's up (or coming down, for that matter!).

# AH-HA 42 PERSONAL DEMONS

Interview congregation members to create a sermon signpost.

## BALLOT BLURB

☐ Put your phone skills to work. You'll interview congregation members and put their answers on signs to create an unforgettable visual for the pastor's sermon.

## SCRIPTURELIFE CONNECTIONS

● Investigate Jesus' ministry, especially when he cast out demons. Read Mark 1:21-34. Ask students: Do demons exist today? With what personal demons do people struggle?

● Spend time with Paul's words in Romans 8:38-39. What things drive a wedge between God and us? What attempts to separate us from God?

## STAFF You'll Need

○ Find a person who enjoys organizing phone-calling.

○ Draw on someone's artistic talent. You'll need a person who can help lead sign-painters.

## STUFF You'll Need

○ church phone directory

○ access to plenty of phones (cell phones included)

○ poster board

○ markers, scissors

○ staples or masking tape to attach signs

○ large free-standing cross as the "signpost"

Begin with a Bible study to grapple with the controversial topic of demons. Use Romans 8:38-39 for starters. Then read about Jesus' miracles in Mark. If students want to dig deeper, find other episodes in the Gospels where Jesus cast out demons.

Pose the question:

• **What are your personal "demons"—whatever tends to separate you from the love of Christ?**

Use a church phone directory to highlight church members to call. Put your phone-callers into action. Write a phone script such as the following: "Hi. My name is [name], and I'm calling for [youth group/church name]. We're calling to get information for the pastor's sermon in a few weeks. The Bible often talked about demons that plagued people. What are the demons you believe plague people today?"

Make sure callers jot down all the replies. Then compare notes and talk about what surprised you. Make a list of words and phrases people mentioned.

Next cut poster board into signs to mount on a large cross, and turn the words and phrases you've collected into poster board signs. Imagine you're creating a giant signpost. (Our poster board signs measured about 3-feet long by 10 inches high, with one end of each sign cut to a point like an arrow.)

Next attach all the signposts to the cross so all the "arrow ends" of the signs point away from the center of the cross. This shows how all the "demons" work to point us away from Jesus. Use this "demon signpost" as a graphic illustration of what separates us from the Lord.

**"UH-OH's"**
(Mistakes WE made, so you don't have to.)

Make sure the signs are legible from a distance. It's easy to forget how far away some people might be, and you want everyone to be able to read the words. Think road signs.

**Our Own "AH-HA's" :-)**

Our pastor used the cross plastered with "bad" signs as a memorable reminder that we all struggle with personal demons. Words such as *pride, money, anger, lying, jealousy, movies,* and *materialism* appeared. People's ears especially perked up when he explained that these were "demons" our own church members identified. The visual portrayal of "sin" signs nailed to the cross powerfully showed how Jesus died for us to deliver us from our "demons."

Our pastor credited our students for calling and getting the information from congregation members. He then had children come forward to read the signs as he explained them in child-friendly language. For example, "*Materialism* means wanting lots of toys." Now that made the topic relevant to all ages!

# WHAT ARE YOU WAITING FOR?

### Find people waiting in line, and videotape what they think about waiting.

## BALLOT BLURB

☐ Grab your video gear, and go on-location where people are "waiting." Find out if there are any similarities between waiting here and waiting for Christ's return.

## SCRIPTURELIFE CONNECTIONS

● Investigate how people handle waiting. Study Matthew 24:42-44. Stop there and discuss what it means to "be ready" here on earth. How does that command make a difference in our everyday lives?

● Dig deeper. Compare these four stories:

1. Matthew 24:45-51 (the difference between the faithful, wise servants and the wicked servants)
2. Matthew 25:1-13 (the parable of the ten virgins)
3. Matthew 25:14-30 (the parable of the talents)
4. Matthew 25:31-46 (separating people like the sheep and the goats)

Form groups of four. (With groups of four, each person can have one story to read). Discuss what all these stories have in common. What is the message for those of us waiting for Christ to return? What advice would you give your friends concerning the truths in these passages?

● Use this experience to talk about patience and impatience. For a glimpse of what's expected of Christians, read Galatians 5:22-23. What does that look like on a day-to-day basis?

## STAFF You'll Need

◯ Recruit someone who can organize students to be video reporters "on the street."

◯ Depending on the size of group, you'll need cars or vans to transport your media crew. Don't forget parents.

## STUFF You'll Need

◯ video cameras, tapes, editing equipment

◯ list of places that are notorious for people having to wait (and maps to get there)

# MAKING IT HAPPEN

Begin with a Bible study on the topic of waiting (or patience). Use Scriptures such as Colossians 3:12 and James 1:2-4.

Develop the questions you'll use for your interview. You might begin with something like this: **"We're doing a video project for our youth group. How do you feel when you have to wait?"**

Make a list of where you plan to interview unsuspecting "waiters." Consider places such as a fast-food drive-through, a popular coffee shop (Starbucks might have a line), a movie theater—you get the picture. Also consider interviewing a pregnant mom. Think of other scenarios that involve waiting in your community. Get creative. Decide who will run the video camera and who will be the asker, and head out.

Once you've collected examples, bring the group together to edit your masterpiece. Make sure to start and end with a humorous clip. Use the "waiting video" as a sermon launcher during Advent or for a sermon on patience.

**Our Own "AH-HA's" :-)**

This project got a lot of laughs because so many people can relate to waiting in line. We did a more "serious" interview of an expectant mother, who gave the kids a great perspective on how their own parents may have felt waiting for them to be born.

We did uncover an actor in our group. Justin introduced the entire "waiting" video as a cooking chef waiting for a pot to boil. Plus, he sat on a park bench conversing with bronze sculpture-people "waiting" on the bench. Justin's debut surprised his parents. You never know what hidden talents might emerge when you do projects like this!

**"UH-OH's"** (Mistakes **we** made, so you don't have to.)

We did make a few impatient people even more aggravated as they waited! Oops! Is there a lesson in that?

# COMMUNION BREAD BAKERS

Work together to make and bake bread
for communion.

## BALLOT BLURB

☐ Want to be a gourmet chef for the Lord? Grab your apron and get in the kitchen. You'll stir up the ingredients to make tasty bread for worship.

## SCRIPTURELIFE CONNECTIONS

● Learn more about "The Bread of Life." Sink your teeth into a Bible study that explores John 6:25-59. After reading the controversial exchange between Jesus and the people, discuss what you believe Jesus was trying to tell them.

● Compare Jesus to bread. If your students have trouble with this concept, read John 6:60 to point out that they're not alone. Even Jesus' disciples said, "This is a hard teaching." Doesn't that make you feel better?

● Study Matthew 6:9-13, The Lord's Prayer, especially, "Give us today our daily bread" in verse 11. What are we praying for when we ask for "daily bread"?

● Chew on the words Jesus used when he warded off temptation in Matthew 4:4. How can those words help us today? Put that story into today's context. What do people hunger for today?

## STAFF You'll Need

◯ Ask someone who loves to bake or cook. This would be an easy, fun way to involve parents who enjoy being in the kitchen.

## STUFF You'll Need

◯ access to an oven (in a home or at church)

◯ ingredients and utensils for the bread (see recipe on p. 105)

# MAKING IT HAPPEN

It's always fun to gather in the kitchen. Before launching into making the bread, you might want to provide an assortment of breads to nibble on while you do the Bible study you chose.

If you already have the ingredients, you can make the bread during this session. Or you may want to meet to decide who'll bring what, and when and where you'll meet to make and bake the bread later.

Decide how many loaves you'll plan to make. (One option is to make a large batch to freeze for future use.) Divide up labor responsibilities, and stir up some fun! Use the recipe at right.

You may want students to help prepare and serve the bread during the worship service for the entire congregation. Or use the bread for a youth worship experience. Or, if you want to go all out, have teenagers design a youth service around the theme of "Jesus, the Bread of Life." They could incorporate discoveries from the Scriptures in their Bible study.

## Lisa's Famous Communion Bread

Melt and heat together:
4 tablespoons butter
¾ cup milk
2 tablespoons honey

Mix in:
1 ½ cup whole wheat flour
½ cup white flour
1 teaspoon salt
1 teaspoon sugar
1 teaspoon baking powder

Mix by hand until well-blended. Take half of mixture and place on floured surface. Knead until it's not grainy (about 1 minute). Roll out to about 1/8-inch thick. Transfer to cookie sheet. Use a pizza cutter to cut into bite-sized pieces. Bake at 375 degrees for 5 minutes. Turn pan in oven and bake another 5 minutes. Cool completely before packaging.
YIELD: Approximately 450 small pieces

## "UH-OH's"
### (Mistakes we made, so you don't have to.)

You may want to experiment with the recipe. There were times we baked it too long and it got too hard and crumbly.

## Our Own "AH-HA's" :-)

In one church we attended, youth made bread for the worship services. Once they started this, some families volunteered to continue making bread for the services. It was a great way to meaningfully involve others in worship preparation.

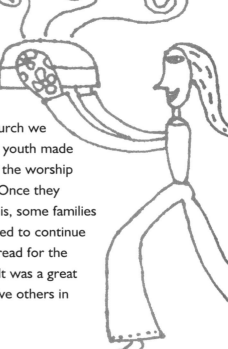

# BONUS SPECIAL EVENT:

# A BAPTISM SCAVENGER HUNT

Use this fun-packed scavenger hunt to dive into baptism. It's a special learning experience, a scavenger hunt, and a celebration all wrapped up into one unforgettable event!

**(You may want to use this blurb to encourage kids to sign up for the event. Include other details such as date, time, and place.)**

**BALLOT BLURB**

☐ **Dive deeper into baptism.** For a day that will make a splash in your life, you'll need your Bible, swimsuit, towel, $5, and a vivid imagination. Sign up now!

## SCRIPTURELIFE CONNECTIONS

● You'll understand baptism like never before through this experiential approach. Each handout (pp. 120-123) lists Scripture references that help complete the scavenger hunt.

## STAFF You'll Need

◯ Recruit someone who's passionate about diving deep into baptism and willing to organize people and places.

◯ Line up drivers with vehicles that can hold a small group of teenagers.

◯ If you include a picnic, find parents to coordinate food and drinks.

◯ Your pastor (optional)

# STUFF You'll Need

## Instructional materials:

◯ typed schedule specific to your time frame and locale for each driver

◯ name, address, and map for each scavenger hunt location for each driver to keep secret

◯ "secret" itinerary unique to each driver

◯ list of attendees so you can prepare personalized washcloths for each (We've also used small T-shirts for newborns.)

◯ copies of each Bible study for each participant (a set given to each driver) (See pages 120-123.)

## Baptism Scavenger Hunt "clue bags":

Create a set of five separate clue bags for each driver, using brown paper sandwich bags. Plan your itinerary, and designate which bag each driver should open first (so not all groups will arrive at the same place at the same time). Clue bags four and five are to be opened fourth and fifth for each group, because everyone will meet together at these locations to eat and swim.

◯ Clue bag one contains one athletic sock (*destination: Laundromat*).

◯ Clue bag two contains enough quarters for a car wash (*destination: car wash*).

◯ Clue bag three contains an adhesive bandage and matches (optional: water wing) (*destination: fire station or pool with rescue divers*).

◯ Clue bag four contains a bottle of water and sand (*destination: park near water*).

◯ Clue bag five contains water balloons (*destination: swimming pool*).

## Opening ceremony supplies:

◯ 1 white washcloth per student with name and baptismal date (if applicable) written on with fabric paint (Check out Wal-Mart for cheap washcloths.)

◯ 1 permanent marker per student

◯ large bowl filled with water

## Closing celebration supplies:

◯ names of person(s) soon to be (or recently) baptized

◯ notecards, envelopes, and writing utensils

## Optional picnic:

◯ "watery" picnic food— for example, submarine sandwiches, bottled water, Chips Ahoy cookies, and other fun theme-related goodies

## Optional follow-up for the event:

◯ clothesline, clothespins, or wooden laundry drying rack

◯ water-themed wrapping paper, ribbon, LifeSavers candies, gift tags

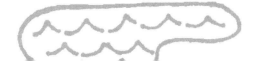

# MAKING IT HAPPEN

If you want to make a lasting impression on kids, plan for this fun, memorable "Baptism Scavenger Hunt." At our church, it has become at least a twice-a-year tradition. It takes some detailed planning and preparation, but it's well worth the extra-mile effort.

Feel free to modify our plan to fit your situation and church traditions. We're just sharing what we've done, which even morphs a bit each time *we* do it. We do know this really works! Kids love it. And years later they can tell us what they learned.

Here's the scoop: Liken the event to a mystery road-trip. Each vehicle (filled with a small group) is given a set of scavenger hunt clue bags containing objects that serve as clues for the baptism destinations. Students must figure out where each clue leads, one destination at a time, and why that destination connects with baptism. The drivers know the destination and drive toward it while the kids are guessing where they're going. Upon arrival, students dive into a special Bible study prepared for that location.

The first time we did this, the date we planned coincided with the local fire and rescue team's practice in a local high school pool. We arranged for the rescue dive team instructor to meet with our kids and explain what it's like to be a rescue worker. He told about what they experience and how they feel in successes and failures. Kids watched scuba divers maneuver blindfolded in and out of an underwater obstacle course. It made the "rescue" point memorable and fascinating.

Since then, we've connected with a local Christian firefighter who enthusiastically embraces our goals. He eagerly awaits our planner's phone call to set up the date. (He even wondered if we had forgotten him when we didn't call as soon as he expected. He really looks forward to sharing his Christian faith with teenagers in this way!)

On his own, he found baptism-themed Bible verses that correspond with different pieces of water-rescue equipment. He hid each piece of equipment with the attached Bible verses. Students had a blast hunting for the equipment throughout the fire station. Then they read their verses out loud and listened to Chris tie his rescue work to baptism. He talked about being saved from death and the devil. He's a wonderful role model and a terrific witness to the youth. Word has it that he's planning to incorporate a practice dive rescue in the lake behind the fire station next time!

# GETTING ORGANIZED

**1. Identify your locations.** You know your area. Figure out the nearest Laundromat, a self-service car wash, a fire station or rescue-diver practice location, a park near water, and a swimming pool. Each location ties to the scavenger hunt and helps teach about baptism.

**2. Make contact with key people at each location** to check for workable dates and times. Explain the program and what to expect. If you need to make reservations for a picnic area or swimming pool, do that, too.

**3. Draw maps to the locations** and include their names, addresses, and phone numbers. Also include your phone number in case of questions along the way. Make copies for each driver. Remember to remind drivers that these are "top secret"—for their eyes only.

**4. Develop a detailed itinerary.** Include schedule times, who's responsible for each area, and when everyone is to meet. Be sure to allow plenty of time for travel and for the activities at each location. Make copies for drivers and any other leaders. Don't hand them to participants. Remember, this is a surprise.

**5. Advertise the event.** Include date, time, what to bring, and cost. Use clip art to make splashy posters or mailings. Tell kids how to register and who to contact.

**6. Collect attendees list.** If applicable, find out kids' baptism dates to include on their personalized washcloths. Buy inexpensive washcloths and a few fabric paint pens. Write each student's name and baptism date on a washcloth. Leave space on the cloths for kids to write five words: one word that describes what they learn at each destination. You'll give a washcloth to each person as kids arrive. You'll collect them at the end of the day to display for the congregation members the following Sunday.

**7. Arrange for drivers.** Parents of participants make a good source of wheels. By the way, this is a great way to involve parents who aren't able to plug in frequently. Not only is it fun, but they'll also learn a lot!

**8. Make up scavenger hunt "clue bags."** Follow the instructions in the "Stuff You'll Need" section. Make one set of bags for each carload of students participating. If you have multiple drivers, set up the first three clue bags so that each driver goes to the locations in a different order. You'll want everyone to wind up together for lunch and the swim party.

**9. Make copies of the Bible study handouts, one for each student.** Have a set ready for each carload so the drivers can hand them out at each destination. You don't want to give away any hints to the location by handing them out too early.

**10. Optional: Arrange for your pastor to join you.** It's a nice touch to have your pastor kick off the event with remarks about baptism. If possible, your pastor could lead the opening ceremony.

**11. Coordinate the picnic.** Delegate food and drink preparation to willing parents. This is another way to involve parents who may be unable to help regularly. See the ideas for water-themed food under "Stuff You'll Need" (on p. 107). Arrange for the parents to be at the park and help serve the picnic. Invite them to stay and listen in on what their kids are learning.

# OPENING CEREMONY

1. **Welcome students as they arrive.** Build anticipation for the scavenger hunt ahead.

2. **Open with prayer.** Hand out a pre-decorated, personalized washcloth to each participant. Gather around a large bowl of water. Depending on your tradition, you may want to gather near the baptismal area of your church.

3. **Give an overview of baptism.** Here are some points we mentioned:
   - Baptism is a gift from God.
   - God commanded that we be baptized.
   - Baptism uses ordinary water combined with an extraordinary promise of entering God's family.
   - Remembering our baptism can give us strength every day.
   - Our baptism scavenger hunt will help us learn more about this special gift.

4. **Experience a baptismal blessing.** Gather around the water. Read Isaiah 43:1-3a. Have students come one by one to the water. Have your pastor or another leader dip a finger in the water and draw a cross on each person's forehead. At the same time, the leader should call each student by name and say, "[Name], you are a child of God." This can be a powerful way for kids to connect with God. It's a real way to experience Isaiah 43:1. Join hands and conclude with prayer. (Feel free to modify or skip this part of the Opening Ceremony if it does not fit well with your own church tradition.)

5. **Get started.** At this time, form small groups that will travel together all day. Have them stand next to the driver as you hand out a set of scavenger hunt clue bags to each carload. Explain that kids are going on a "Baptism Scavenger Hunt" to learn as much about baptism as they can.

Give any last-minute details and answer any questions. Then send kids off!

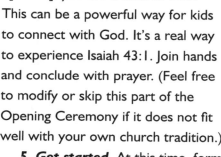

## Our Own "AH-HA's" :-)

The first year we did this, our opening ceremony became extra special. Danny and his family joined us as Danny got baptized. All of us gathered around and celebrated this special occasion. Danny's baptism launched our day, as it launched a new life for him!

# THE BAPTISM SCAVENGER HUNT

During the scavenger hunt, your students will experience these five points:

**1. Baptism cleanses us.** (Do at a Laundromat.) The Laundromat becomes a classroom for reinforcing the cleansing power of baptism. See the Bible study on page 120.

**2. Baptism brings forgiveness.** (Do at a car wash.) Watch a car wash brush away old ideas of classrooms. Not only do kids connect the power of forgiveness with baptism, but they also act as servants to clean their drivers' car. See how the Bible study on page 121 connects.

**3. Baptism rescues us.** (Do at a fire station or rescue diver location.) Use your local fire station or rescue dive location to teach the power of rescuing. Depending on your location, you can honor local rescue staff by having them share their knowledge. The Bible study on page 122 helps tie it all together.

**4. Baptism is power.** (Do at a park near water—a river, lake, whatever.) Look for ways to tie the power of baptism into your location. Use the Bible study on page 123.

**5. Baptism is a reason to celebrate.** Here's where you can party! Since the earlier part of the day is quite structured, let kids play now. Use laughter and fun to teach that the church can have a great time because of what God has done for us in baptism!

Here's where drivers felt it was worthwhile to volunteer. Kids hopped out of the vehicle and washed the car with the quarters found in the clue bag. We enjoyed seeing the surprise on their faces when they finally guessed that the quarters were the clue to a car wash.

After having a great time scrubbing the car—and amusing the driver with this unexpected gift—kids huddled together in the vehicle to do the Bible study. They proudly wrote "Forgiven" on their washcloths, anticipating the next destination.

We journeyed up a nearby mountain canyon to a park that originally housed a power plant. Because a catastrophic flood wiped out the power plant years ago, we were reminded of the power of floodwaters. If your community has experienced flood damage, you may want to pick a place with a similar history.

A number of plaques commemorating the flood had been placed around the park. We actually held a walking Bible study from plaque to plaque and tied it to our Bible readings.

This park made a great picnic spot, too.

# CLOSING CEREMONY

**1. Gather for a final prayer.**
Once everyone joins at the final location, form a circle and recap what students have learned so far. Have kids write "celebrate" on their washcloths and hand them back to you. Tell them to be on the lookout for where the washcloths will appear.

**2. Celebrate a new baptism.** If you know of someone who is soon to be baptized, have students write a note to that person, offering a prayer for him or her.

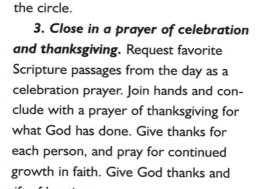

Kids can mention some of the things they learned today to include in the cards. Gather the cards in the center of the circle.

**3. Close in a prayer of celebration and thanksgiving.** Request favorite Scripture passages from the day as a celebration prayer. Join hands and conclude with a prayer of thanksgiving for what God has done. Give thanks for each person, and pray for continued growth in faith. Give God thanks and praise for the gift of baptism.

**4. Take a dive!** Send everyone off to the pool for fun. Give any last instructions, and thank everyone for coming.

## Our Own "AH-HA's" :-)

We used the public indoor recreation center's pool for our grand finale. To our amazement, our kids were unashamed to join for prayer in the public lobby. There we sat with our washcloths, notecards, and circle of prayer. Their spirit of community and friendship witnessed that they weren't embarrassed to pray in public and proudly profess their faith.

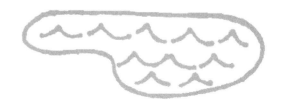

# FOLLOW-UP FUN

**1. Hang-ups.** After you've collected all the washcloths, go back to church and string a clothesline where people walk into worship. Clothespin all the washcloths to the line for all to see. It's a great representation of what you experienced during your "Baptism Scavenger Hunt." If you don't want to use a clothesline, a wooden laundry-drying rack works too. This really gets people talking!

**2. Gift-wrapped reminders.** In the next week, take down the washcloths, and wrap each one as a reminder of the day. Add a ribbon with a LifeSavers candy attached. Include a note that says "Jesus loves you and is your lifesaver!"

**3. LifeSavers thank-you's.** To thank all the drivers and other helpers, give each person a roll of LifeSavers candies with a note saying, "Thanks for all your help with our "Baptism Scavenger Hunt"! You were a lifesaver!"

**4. Next time!** Begin planning your next baptism special event. Evaluate what worked well and what needs to be improved.

## Our Own "AH-HA's" :-)

We are blessed to have an adult, Leslie, who is passionate about this special event. For three years she has volunteered to plan these events because they've become so meaningful in the lives of kids—and adults. Each time, she has modified the event to fit the size of the group and time of year. (Note the "Fall Fun" box on page 114.) Leslie has even taken time to do this event in small groups and one-on-one if necessary to accommodate kids' schedules. Now that's dedication!

We heard another great story (by accident) the last time the entry area showcased the baptism "hang-ups." This time newborn T-shirts hung from the clothesline. People gazed upward, intrigued, commenting on how good the decorated shirts looked. Then a woman saw us and asked if the clothesline would be staying up for a while. She hoped so. That was because one of the last times we did this, she brought a visitor to church who was so touched by the sight that she still talks about it today. It really impacted her.

# FALL FUN

Fall sparked another baptism connection and fun activity. Everyone designed a Christian symbol to carve on a pumpkin. Before launching into the activity, kids heard this comparison:

*A newly baptized person compared herself to a pumpkin. She likened herself to a dirty pumpkin in a patch. She was a dusty, unappealing pumpkin that God had handpicked and washed clean. She described her new life as if God had taken the top off a pumpkin and pulled out all the slimy, yucky stuff inside. Not only that but God also removed the seeds of doubt, hate, greed, and jealousy. Once those were gone, he carved a smile on her face for Christ's light to shine through.*

Kids discussed how a lighted carved pumpkin demonstrates the meaning of baptism.

Our Own "AH-HA's" :-)

Because this day became part of our kids' portfolios of learning, the day began with a baptism pretest. Before the closing celebration, students completed the same test again. In this way we measured how much students learned that day.

**weblink** Get Graphics & Ballot Blurbs **Online!**
Designing your own ballots? Go to **www.grouppublishing.com/ creativefaithahhas/ballotextras** to download the illustrations used in this book as well as the ballot blurbs for all 45 Ah-Ha's.

CREATIVE FAITH AH-HAS!

HANDOUTS

# Help us make an **awesome** symbol of our congregation!

Please use this pattern to make a cross that represents your family. You can use fabric or other lightweight material. We will glue it to our church banner to show the diversity of the body of Christ. (That means your cross will become a permanent part of the banner and you won't be able to get it back.)

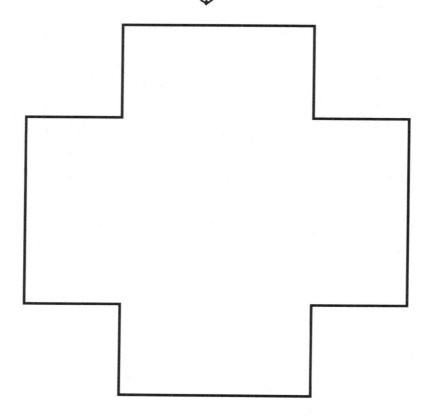

**P**lease return your special cross no later than

_____
(date).

**B**ring your cross to our collection place:

------------------------------------
(place).

**Thank you for helping our youth picture the body of Christ in our midst.**

# Christian Career Paths

Next week you'll get to meet real people who do real ministry jobs. That'll be really fun! So choose three Christian careers you would like to learn more about. Check three only.

CAREER LADDER

_____ Pastor

_____ Director of Christian Education/Youth Ministry/Family Ministry

_____ Director of Music Ministry

_____ Director of Outreach Ministry

_____ Christian Schoolteacher

Name:

_____

_____

**WATCH FOR DETAILS NEXT WEEK.**

**YOU'LL GET YOUR VERY OWN SCHEDULE SO YOU'LL KNOW WHOM YOU'LL MEET AND WHEN.**

**SEE YOU NEXT WEEK!**

# We Need

Help us collect food items for special food baskets. Our youth group will deliver them to families in need. Thank you for your help.

_pasta

_rice

_canned fruit

_canned vegetables

_tomato sauce

_baking mixes

_cereal

_flour

_peanut butter

_soup

_macaroni and cheese

_crackers

_baby food

_baby formula

# Baptism
# Cleanses Us
## Welcome to the Laundromat!

### This place reminds us that we are made new and clean through baptism.
## The old dies with Christ.

**1.** How does a Laundromat remind us of baptism?

**2.** When have you ever buried your clothes? (Here's a clue: Have you ever hidden clothes under your bed or in your closet?)

**3.** Read Romans 6:3-5. From these verses, what does baptism have to do with being buried?

**4.** How is baptism like washing germs and odors away? Check Acts 22:16.

**5.** Read Galatians 3:27. What do these words say about new, clean clothes?

**6.** Read Mark 16:16. When have you tried too long to keep old clothes you really like? Can they be saved after they've been ruined with dirt and grime? How is that like or unlike people?

**7.** Figure out an easy way to remember Ephesians 4:5. Together invent a Laundromat/baptismal cheer to remember this verse. Write it here:

**8.** Write "cleansed" on your washcloth as a reminder of baptism washing away the old you and making you new in Christ.

**CLEANSED**

# Baptism Brings Forgiveness

Hey! You've made it to the car wash!

Find out how baptism brings the
## cleansing of forgiveness into our lives.

1. Have you washed your driver's vehicle? Be sure to thank that person for taking the time to be with you and serve you in this way.

2. What are the ways the dirt on the cars is like sin in our lives?

3. Who has sinned? Read Romans 3:23.

4. What happened to our sin in baptism? Read Acts 22:16.

5. How is this car wash like baptism?

6. Read Titus 3:5-7. Why is baptism a "washing of rebirth"?

7. What does it mean to you that your sins are washed away through baptism?

8. Write "forgiven" on your washcloth.

1. When was a time you desperately needed help? How did you feel?

2. How is baptism like being rescued from a desperate situation?

3. Read Colossians 1:13-14 and Colossians 2:12-14. What words in those verses mean the most to you personally? Why?

4. What about the dive and rescue information reminds you most of baptism?

# Baptism
# Rescues
## Us

5. Write "rescued" on your washcloth.

# Baptism Is Power!

**1.** Where can you see the power of water? When have you ever experienced the power of water?

**2.** Examine Jesus' baptism. Read Luke 3:21-22. Notice the words God uses as he refers to his Son. How do you feel knowing God claims you as his child in baptism too? How do you sense power in those words?

**3.** Read Mark 1:4-11. Where is "baptism" power in these verses?

**4.** Read Matthew 28:18-20. Where is "baptism" power in these verses?

**5.** Read Colossians 2:12 and Romans 6:3-5. Where is "baptism" power in these verses?

**6.** Look around you. Do you see any evidence of water's power? Have you ever had a flooding experience? If so, tell about it. Now read 1 Peter 3:18-22. How was the flood in Noah's time like baptism?

**7.** Write "power" on your washcloth.

# ACTIVITY MATRIX

The 45 Ah-Ha's in this book involve a wide variety of activities that appeal to the many unique talents and aptitudes of teenagers. Use this matrix to select some Ah-Ha's that are a perfect match for the students in your ministry!

| Activity | Ah-Ha 1 | Ah-Ha 2 | Ah-Ha 3 | Ah-Ha 4 | Ah-Ha 5 | Ah-Ha 6 | Ah-Ha 7 | Ah-Ha 8 | Ah-Ha 9 | Ah-Ha 10 | Ah-Ha 11 | Ah-Ha 12 | Ah-Ha 13 | Ah-Ha 14 | Ah-Ha 15 |
|---|---|---|---|---|---|---|---|---|---|---|---|---|---|---|---|
| Writing | | | | | | | | | | | | | | | |
| Video Production | ✕ | | | | | | | | | | | | | | |
| Travel | ✕ | | | | | | | | | ✕ | | ✕ | | | |
| Photography | | | | | | | | | | ✕ | | ✕ | ✕ | | |
| Organizing or Research | | | | | | | | | | | ✕ | | | | |
| Music | | ✕ | | | ✕ | | | | ✕ | | | | | | |
| Interviewing | ✕ | | | | | | | | | | ✕ | | | | |
| Electronics and Technology | ✕ | | | | | | ✕ | | | ✕ | | ✕ | | | |
| Drama or Up-front Action | | | | ✕ | | ✕ | | | ✕ | | | | | | |
| Dance | | | | | | | | | | | | | | | |
| Construction and Design | | | | | | | ✕ | | | | | | | ✕ | |
| Baking | | | | | | | | | | | | | | | |
| Art and Crafts | | | ✕ | | | | | ✕ | | | | | | | ✕ |

**Activity Titles:**

- Ah-Ha 1: On-the-Street Doubters (p. 16)
- Ah-Ha 2: Be Instrumental (p. 18)
- Ah-Ha 3: Keepsake Creations (p. 20)
- Ah-Ha 4: In the Spotlight (p. 22)
- Ah-Ha 5: Music Makers (p. 24)
- Ah-Ha 6: Puppet Players (p. 26)
- Ah-Ha 7: Puppet Players Support Team (p. 28)
- Ah-Ha 8: Puppet Creators (p. 30)
- Ah-Ha 9: Silent Singers (p. 32)
- Ah-Ha 10: Phenomenal Photographers (p. 34)
- Ah-Ha 11: Research Specialists (p. 36)
- Ah-Ha 12: Foto Fun Prayer (p. 38)
- Ah-Ha 13: Photo Gallery of God's People in Action (p. 40)
- Ah-Ha 14: Prayer Wall Construction Team (p. 42)
- Ah-Ha 15: Thanksgiving Prayer Chain (p. 44)

## ACTIVITY MATRIX

The 45 Ah-Ha's in this book involve a wide variety of activities that appeal to the many unique talents and aptitudes of teenagers. Use this matrix to select some Ah-Ha's that are a perfect match for the students in your ministry!

| Category | Ah-Ha 16: Growing Globe Surprise (p. 46) | Ah-Ha 17: Make Headlines (p. 48) | Ah-Ha 18: Artists' Corner (p. 50) | Ah-Ha 19: Spy Cam (p. 52) | Ah-Ha 20: Calling All Carpenters (p. 54) | Ah-Ha 21: Worship in Motion (p. 56) | Ah-Ha 22: Butterfly Factory (p. 58) | Ah-Ha 23: Easter Cross in Bloom (p. 60) | Ah-Ha 24: Body-of-Christ Banner Bunch (p. 62) | Ah-Ha 25: Thanksgiving Mural Mania (p. 64) | Ah-Ha 26: Responsive Prayers (p. 66) | Ah-Ha 27: Christmas Angels (p. 68) | Ah-Ha 28: Christmas Angel Video Documentary (p. 70) | Ah-Ha 29: Designer Bulletin Covers (p. 72) | Ah-Ha 30: Church Improvement (p. 74) | Ah-Ha 31: Christian Career Paths (p. 76) |
|---|---|---|---|---|---|---|---|---|---|---|---|---|---|---|---|---|
| Writing | | X | | | | | | | | | X | | | | | |
| Video Production | | | | X | | | | | | | | | X | | | |
| Travel | | | | | | | | | | | | X | X | | | |
| Photography | | | | | | | | | | | | | | | | |
| Organizing or Research | | X | | | | | | X | X | | | X | | | | |
| Music | | | | | | | | | | | | | | | | |
| Interviewing | | X | | | | | | | | | | X | | | | X |
| Electronics and Technology | | | | X | | | | | | | X | | X | | | |
| Drama or Up-front Action | | | | | | X | | | | | | | | | | |
| Dance | | | | | | X | | | | | | | | | | |
| Construction and Design | X | | | | X | | | | | | | | | X | | |
| Baking | | | | | | | | | | | | | | | | |
| Art and Crafts | X | X | | | | | X | X | X | X | X | | | X | | |

## ACTIVITY MATRIX

The 45 Ah-Ha's in this book involve a wide variety of activities that appeal to the many unique talents and aptitudes of teenagers. Use this matrix to select some Ah-Ha's that are a perfect match for the students in your ministry!

**Activity Key**

- Ah-Ha 32: Stuff John! (p. 78)
- Ah-Ha 33: Giant Treasure Chest (p. 80)
- Ah-Ha 34: Glitter and Gold Gift Bags (p. 82)
- Ah-Ha 35: Tele-thankers (p. 84)
- Ah-Ha 36: Prayer Path Prep (p. 86)
- Ah-Ha 37: Prayer Path Promotions (p. 90)
- Ah-Ha 38: Spirited Mobile (p. 92)
- Ah-Ha 39: Food Baskets for the Needy (p. 94)
- Ah-Ha 40: Music Video Makers (p. 96)
- Ah-Ha 41: Raising the Roof by Lowering a Friend (p. 98)
- Ah-Ha 42: Personal Demons (p. 100)
- Ah-Ha 43: What Are You Waiting For? (p. 102)
- Ah-Ha 44: Communion Bread Bakers (p. 104)
- Ah-Ha 45: Bonus Special Event: A Baptism Scavenger Hunt (p. 106)

| Category | 32 | 33 | 34 | 35 | 36 | 37 | 38 | 39 | 40 | 41 | 42 | 43 | 44 | 45 |
|---|---|---|---|---|---|---|---|---|---|---|---|---|---|---|
| Writing | | | | | | | | | | | | | | |
| Video Production | | | | | | | | | X | | | X | | |
| Travel | | | | | | | | | | | | X | | X |
| Photography | | | | | | | | | X | | | | | |
| Organizing or Research | | | | | | X | | | | | X | | | |
| Music | | | | | | | | | X | | | | | |
| Interviewing | | | | X | | | | | X | | X | X | | X |
| Electronics and Technology | | | | X | X | | | | | | | X | | |
| Drama or Up-front Action | | | | | | | | | | X | | | | |
| Dance | | | | | | | | | | | | | | |
| Construction and Design | X | | | | X | | | | | X | | | | |
| Baking | | | | | | | | | | | | | X | |
| Art and Crafts | X | X | X | | X | | X | | | | X | | | X |

# Scripture Index

## *Old Testament*

## *New Testament*

# Seasonal/Theme Index

Here's another way to choose Creative Faith Ah-Ha's! Review this list for Bible studies, theme ideas, or ideas for the church seasons.
"There is a time for everything, and a season for every activity under heaven" (Ecclesiastes 3:1).